D0148227

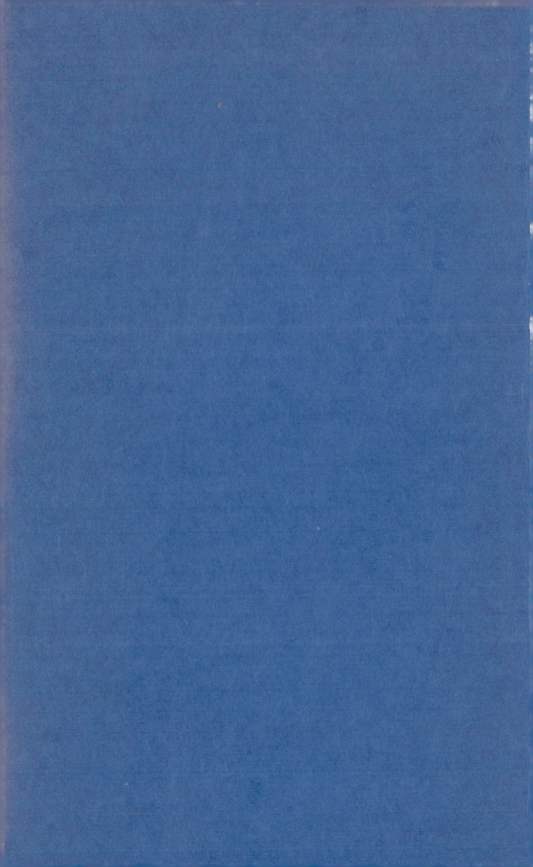

Interpreting Kant

B 2798 .I56 1982

Interpreting Kant

Interpreting
KANT

Edited with Introduction by

MOLTKE S. GRAM

University of Iowa Press Ψ Iowa City

RITTER LIBRARY
BALDWIN-WALLACE COLLEGE
WITHDRAWN

University of Iowa Press, Iowa City 52242
© *1982 by The University of Iowa. All rights reserved*
Printed in the United States of America

Library of Congress Cataloging in Publication Data

Main entry under title:

Interpreting Kant.

    Includes bibliographical references and index.
    Contents: Is sensation the matter of appearances? /
Richard Aquila — Vorstellung and Erkenntnis in Kant /
Rolf George — The sense of a Kantian intuition / Moltke S.
Gram — [etc.]
    1. Kant, Immanuel, 1724 – 1804 — Addresses, essays,
lectures.   I. Gram, Moltke S.
B2798.I56 1982   193   82 – 13627
ISBN 0 – 87745 – 118 – 4

TO
LEWIS WHITE BECK
Nestor of American Kant Scholarship

Contents

Text, Translation, and Tradition

What appears here is the outgrowth of the symposium on the relation between philology and philosophy in the Kantian tradition held at the 1980 meetings of the American Philosophical Association (Eastern Division). The original symposium was jointly sponsored by the Committee on International Co-operation of that association and the Thyssen *Stiftung*. The present volume breaks new ground: It is the first unified attempt to explore this area. I do not attempt here to catalog the contents of the individual contributions to the volume. They speak for themselves. Instead, I offer a framework within which they can be understood as a unity.

The present volume is not an exercise in lexicography. No appeal to the dictionary can solve the problems that face the tradition of Kant scholarship here. Kant's German usage, as we shall see, often diverges from the standard, received German of his time. But traditional and Kantian contexts of usage nonetheless overlap, and this generates the overriding problem of interpretation. Sharp semantical divergences in the use of the same linguistic expression can be detected without recourse to philosophical exegesis of the text. But semantical overlap demands such an exegesis if we are to determine the points at which the divergence occurs. And this in turn involves a philosophical inquiry into the place of the expression within the structure of Kant's argument. Thus the need for the integration of philology and philosophy into philosophical semantics. This is also what makes the present undertaking distinctive. Consider the major examples which are treated in what follows.

(1) First, the Kantian notion of a sensation (*Empfindung*). Is it the matter of perception? Or do spatio-temporal objects constitute that

matter? Kant equivocates. At A167 = B208-9 of the first *Kritik*, he affirms the former. But at B147 of the same work, he claims the latter, saying that spatio-temporal objects are the matter of perception while sensations merely accompany this perception. Thus sensation may be a means by which we perceive objects. They may also become occasionally objects of perception. But they are not the matter of perception.

The issue here is signalled by a semantical shift in the use of *Empfindung*, which can be clarified only by a philosophical inspection of the place of that term in Kant's theory of perception. If you say that sensations are the immediate objects and hence the matter of perception, then you have the problem of relating them to the objects which are responsible for their occurrence in our respective sensory fields. The only relation available within Kant's theory is causal. But the application of the causal axiom to the relation between sensation understood as the matter of perception and the object which is supposedly responsible for our experience of it involves the illegitimate use of that axiom to relate things to themselves to what appears to us under our forms of intuition. And it glaringly clashes with Kant's claim that things in themselves are not causes.

If you choose to say that spatio-temporal objects and not sensations are the matter of perception, you escape one difficulty only to face another. You have the problem of what Kant calls "appearance." *Erscheinung* can be rendered into English as "sensation" or, perhaps, "sensum," or—what is even more dubious—"impression." The problem now becomes the relation of the matter of appearance to appearances. And the solution of this problem assumes clarity about the relation of a sensation to an appearance. The dictionaries cannot decide the issue. There must be an appeal to the sense of the term within Kant's own theory.

(2) The problem which *Empfindung* raises can be generalized by reference to the notion of a Kantian representation (*Vorstellung*). Whether sensation is the matter of perception can now be raised with respect to any object of representation whatever. The issue, then, is this. What is the relation between what Kant calls the matter of intuition—whether it is an appearance or a sensation—and a representation, which is how Kant designates the object of every mental act? If anything can count as a representation that can be the object of a mental act, then is the concept of a representation exhaustively specified by enumerating all of the possible objects of our mental acts? Is it, in other words, a variable ranging over terms for sensations,

impressions, appearances, and their relatives? Or is it, rather, a special kind of object itself?

Neither alternative escapes initial difficulty. If you opt for the former rendering of "representation," then what Kant calls a *Vorstellung* is any disjunct of the total disjunctive array consisting of terms which designate possible objects of mental acts. To say that an object is a representation would not, on this alternative, imply that a representation is an object. But this would break down on the stubborn fact that there are representations that have no objects. Sensations may, for example, on occasion *be* objects of mental acts. But they do not *have* objects. And we can think of objects which do not exist. The first rendering of "representation" fails to explain the relation of these facts to our mental acts.

The second alternative initially fares no better. Suppose that a representation is a kind of object among other objects. This would admittedly find an ontological shelter for mental acts which have as objects things that do not exist. But it would not explain the relation between the notion of a representation when it is applied to these objects and to that notion when it is applied to other objects. A non-existent object can be a representation in the same sense as an object that exists without illegitimately insinuating the notion of an existent object into the specification of an object that does not exist. That is the dilemma which threatens the semantical integrity of a Kantian *Vorstellung*.

(3) Kant's notion of intuition (*Anschauung*) perpetuates these philosophical-cum-philological difficulties. We are told that something is to count as an intuition just in case it is an immediate object of consciousness. But this leaves it open whether that notion can be explicated in terms of, say, *Empfindung*, or any of the other terms that Kant uses to botanize the flora of our mental lives. If you take this way out, the account of what an intuition is that you will be imputing to Kant will be circular. The notions of sensation and appearance assume the notion of an intuition. Their referents are all instances of intuitions. It may be true that intuitions are sensations, appearances, or impressions. But this does not imply that what is true of an intuition is part of what it is to *be* an intuition.

The other alternative is no less troublesome. Suppose that we try to account for what a Kantian intuition is independently of reference to the possible objects of mental acts which would make such an account circular. This would apparently require us to define "intuition" independently of any form of intuition whatever. The forms of

Kantian intuition are, as we know, one and all contingent facts about our sensory apparatus. None of them can tell us what an intuition essentially is. It can only give us a further instance of an intuition. But if the notion of a Kantian intuition is to be defined independently of *any* form of intuition at all, any successful definition would merely tell us something about how things which are in principle not objects of possible experience are immediately present to consciousness. And this is a contradiction in terms.

(4) The problems continue. Kant's use of *Erkenntnis* (knowledge) gives us a problem with two alternative but mutually incompatible solutions. The symptom is philological. The root, philosophical. Take them in turn. What Kant calls *Erkenntnis* is ambiguous. The verbal form, *erkennen,* can take either a direct object or a dependent clause. We can say that somebody knows the location of a city. But we can also say that he knows that the city in question is large. This ambiguity is inherent in the tradition. And Kant preserves it. The result of this is philosophically problematic. The first sense of the word indicates that knowledge is not judgmental. *Erkenntnis* is a term in judgment but not the judgment itself. The second sense gives us a case of cognition but not of knowledge.

Kant wavers here. He tells us sometimes that *Erkenntnis* can be divided into singular and general terms. He confirms this at other places. He says that judgment is just the connection of cognitions (*cognitiones* or *Erkenntnisse*). But then he says that a judgment is an act by which representations must become cognitions of an object. This suggests that we must distinguish between knowledge and something like cognition. All cognitions are expressed by sentences with expressions for direct objects. All cases of knowledge are expressed by sentences with expressions for states of affairs or facts.

The recommendation has some independent evidence in its ability to illuminate the otherwise obscure transition in Kant's argument in the Transcendental Analytic of the first *Kritik*. There Kant first draws up a list of what he calls concepts of various kinds of properties of judgment *überhaupt*. He then draws up a table of concepts which he calls concepts of an object in general. The former are concepts which are about the objects of judgment. The problem: Kant claims that the latter is derivable from the former when, on the face of it, the two tables of concepts are about very different domains. If we read *Erkenntnis* as "cognition" and not "knowledge," then we might be able to explain how Kant could draw what would otherwise be an invalid conclusion. If *Erkenntnis* here is a case of cognition and not knowledge, then all the concepts which are listed in Kant's "Table of the Forms of the Unity of Thought in Judgment" are referential; hence, the transition from one table to another is no more than an emphasis on two aspects of one and the same set of concepts.

But the distinction between cognition and knowledge is both philosophically and philologically fickle. You can appeal to the same distinction in order to make the difference between metaphysical and transcendental knowledge intelligible. Kant calls any case of knowledge transcendental whenever it is about what he calls the mode of our cognition *(Erkenntnisart)* of objects. Knowledge is metaphysical whenever it pertains to the objects themselves. One might argue that the distinction demands a corresponding distinction between cognition and knowledge. Knowledge pertains to the way in which we grasp the latter. The issue here is whether the distinction between metaphysical and transcendental knowledge demands a corresponding distinction between cognition and knowledge. And it turns on whether a conflation of cognition with knowledge would make the two kinds of knowledge indistinguishable from each other. If we adopt the former alternative, then we need the distinction in order to make a transition which, on the latter alternative, would obliterate the distinction between transcendental and metaphysical knowledge.

(5) The issue facing our understanding of a Kantian *Erkenntnis* is duplicated within the context of the Table of Categories itself. *Erkenntnis* gives us the problem of distinguishing between two kinds of knowledge: One, of the concepts of the logical structure of a judgment; the other, of objects. The Table of Categories contains both the concept of a pervasive characteristic of objects in a manifold and a concept of a characteristic of the concepts by means of which we synthesize those objects. Kant calls the former the categories of quality and the latter categories of modality. In both cases he discusses what has come to be translated as "existence" but for which there are two separate words in the German. The relevant category of quality is the concept of reality *(Realität)*; that of the relevant category of modality, actuality or existence *(Wirklichkeit* or *Dasein)*. The issue is whether these two terms have the same or different senses. Kant's famous hundred-thaler example in his refutation of the Ontological Argument supposedly demands the recognition of two very different senses which are often disastrously concealed behind one word. Consider how this comes about.

Kant's version of the Ontological Argument has its advocate claiming, notoriously, that existence is a predicate. Kant faults this, allegedly, by an example: The one hundred thalers that exist contain no more determinations than a hundred thalers that do not exist. The conclusion is as well known as its premises: The Ontological Argument collapses because every predication of existence is synthetic and not analytic; hence, existence is not a predicate and the Ontological Argument falls to the ground.

The substitution of "real" for "actual" in Kant's example would threaten to traduce the entire argument. For one thing, the substitution would make the hundred-thaler example question-begging. Both Kant and his opponents can agree that what we conceive whenever we form a determinate concept of something is real. But they disagree about whether what we thus conceive is actual. Should the two terms be conflated, then whatever is real is actual. The opposition wins. And, what is even worse, both parties to the dispute can agree that we can form a concept of something and still not know whether it is actual. But this is a fact about the limitation of our state of enlightenment about all of the predicates that are packed into a concept, not about whether existence or actuality is in fact a predicate or not.

For another, the hundred-thaler example is viable only if there is a genuine distinction between a real and logical use of a predicate. Substition of "real" for "actual" would obliterate that distinction. Kant does not deny that "exists" is a predicate. He claims only that it is a logical, not a real, predicate. But if we conflate the actual with the real, there is no basis for the claim that existence or actuality is not a real predicate. The foundation for the distinction between real and logical predicates, then, is the more fundamental distinction between actuality and reality. We can construct a concept of anything — from which it analytically follows that whatever we conceive by means of that concept is real. It does not, however, follow that what we conceive is actual. Kant's example begs the question only on the assumption that existence or actuality is a real rather than a logical predicate.

Other evidence reinforces this conclusion. There is a difference between what Kant does with the concept of reality in the Anticipations and the concept of actuality or existence in the Postulates. To ignore the distinction between actuality and reality makes it impossible to explain why Kant undertakes to demonstrate the applicability to two different concepts to our experience of objects. The argument in the Anticipations is supposed to prove that every intuition has an intensive magnitude. The argument in the Postulates, however, purports to demonstrate that there exist things outside us. The former argument applies equally to dream and to waking states. The latter does not. Obliterating the distinction between reality and actuality would make the latter proof superfluous.

Suppose, then, that we see ourselves forced to honor the distinction between reality and actuality. There is still a residual problem with this gambit. We are left with a distinction within the Table of Categories between those concepts which refer to objects of experience and those which refer to the concepts we have of those objects. This generates two conflicting accounts of what it is to be a Kantian category. Such a concept is about an object of possible experience. It is nevertheless a concept of a concept. And this threatens the distinction Kant makes between the Table of Functions of Unity of Thought in Judgment and the Table of Categories.

(6) Kant distinguishes between *Wille* (legislative will) and *Willkür* (elective will). This, like its predecessors, visits both a philological and a philosophical problem on us. Philological, because the sense of the two expressions is no clearer in the original than it is without elaborate paraphrase in an English translation. Philosophical, because an inability to draw a distinction between them fatally cripples Kant's theory of moral agency. The problem has a simple but shady background. We make choices among various alternative possible ends. All free (spontaneous) human agency is action according to what Kant calls either a hypothetical or a categorical imperative. We are to understand both kinds of imperative in terms of the more general notion of what it is to will any end. We can will an end because of a motive which is entirely contingent upon the desires of the agent. But we can also will an end because it is enjoined upon us irrespective of the happenstantial desires or drives (*Triebe*) we may have. Both kinds of motive are grounds of choice (*Beweggründe*). But does that ground of choice lie in *Wille* or *Willkür*?

A troublesome ambiguity in the notion of *Willkür* complicates all of this. Both the German original and the English equivalent of that expression can be understood as meaning either "to lack reason" or "to require no further reason." The former sense of *Willkür* implies that any action initiated by an agent is arbitrary. The former, that any such action is based on an ultimate reason. The philological blur begets a major philosophical perplexity. The basic sense of Kantian *Willkür* is the ability to choose among alternative ends. This is neutral with respect to either of the two senses of *Willkür* that make trouble for Kant's theory of moral agency.

But the neutrality is forfeit once the theory is viewed under the more microscopic light of the ambiguity residing in the notion of *Willkür*. If that term is supposed to denote any act that lacks reason, then the motive that animates the performance of the act is subject to the causal axiom: What is chosen is the result of a cause external to the will and is therefore not free. We may try to avoid this consequence by rendering *Willkür* as what is applicable to any action the motive of which is not based on a more ultimate reason. But this escapes one difficulty only to invite another. This would make any action that is chosen by *Willkür* an action of *Wille*. And this would transform the notion of *Willkür* into a characterization of any action that is freely chosen. The distinction between a legislative and an elective will would deliquesce.

The problem, then, is this. The concept of willing any end includes the concepts of willing something as an effect of your action and of willing whatever means are necessary to bring that effect about. If what Kant calls *Willkür* accounts for this, then what he calls *Wille* would seem to be superfluous. If *Wille* does this, then *Willkür* would seem to be superfluous. And this is not the least of the problem. If you say with Kant that *Willkür* is the faculty of elective will, then you provide only another description of the legislative will. And if you deny this in order to preserve the distinction between *Wille* and *Willkür*, then you succeed only in distinguishing between an act which is governed by the causal axiom and an act which is not so governed. The dilemma remains in either case. If *Willkür* is the faculty of choice, then all morally responsible action would seem to be subject to the causal axiom and therefore not free. But if *Wille* assumes the task of that faculty, then there is no need for the distinction between *Wille* and *Willkür* at all.

(7) The preservation of Kant's distinctions both in and out of the Germanic linguistic tradition continue to face semantical conflation. He distinguishes between what he calls *Zweck* (purpose or end) and *Zweckmäßigkeit* (purposiveness). The latter makes trouble. Both can be glossed as so many cases of finality. But the usage suffers from ambiguity. *Zweck* or "finality" can mean either "decisive" or "ultimate." But it can also mean "the end stage of a temporal process." One ambiguity begets another. Once we have uncovered the first, we inherit the problem of translating *Zweck* in such adjectival forms as *zwecklos*. If we prefer to say that whatever is to count as a *Zweck* is the end stage of a temporal process, then it is possible to render to count anything as *zwecklos* that is without an end stage.

The semantical ambiguity is philosophically important. It invites the question about whether there are things that lack an end but are not without purpose. The worrisome fact remains: There are instances of finality that are ultimate but not the end stage of a temporal process. And there are temporal processes without end. The confirmation or verification of empirical propositions is an instance of the latter. Fallibilism semantically canonizes that fact. But there are also instances of an activity of a natural kind when it has achieved its proper end. Aristotle's example of the acorn whose telic factor is to become an oak is a banal but convincing example of this kind of finality.

If we understand "purposiveness" as "having no temporal end," then we deprive ourselves of any chance of understanding what Kant means when he claims that there are things in the world which are purposive but which do not have purpose (*Zweckmäßigkeit ohne Zweck*). Antecedent commitments to the understanding of *Zweck* rule out the possibility that what is purpose without a purpose may, after all, have a purpose which we cannot ascertain.

This, however, accompanies an even greater difficulty. Natural objects like Aristotle's acorn are capable of achieving a state at the conclusion of a temporal process. But if this description were to be applied to art objects, we would succeed only in assimilating them to natural objects. And this would make it impossible for Kant or anybody else to distinguish between something that has an end from anything that is purposive without a purpose having an end.

We are now in a position to take preliminary and provisional stock. We have canvassed an inventory of difficulties which face anybody who wants to make sense out of Kant's theories. None of these problems is to be encountered in the ordinary course of translation. Each of the key terms we have been examining here presents a problem which cannot be solved by purely philological inquiries. Every one of them has two alternative renderings, each of which is plausible but faces serious philosophical problems. Review them in turn.

The notion of *Empfindung* is customarily rendered as "sensation," with the understanding that it is what Kant calls the matter of perception. But, as we have seen, packing this into the notion of a Kantian *Empfindung* involves the application of the causal axiom to something that is not an object of possible human experience. And, as we have also seen, *Empfindung* can be removed from the position of being the matter of perception only at the prohibitive cost of a substitution that seems to inherit the very problem it was supposed to solve.

A Kantian *Vorstellung* fares no better. If it is an object among objects of possible awareness, we cannot account for the sense in which sensations, appearances, and whatever else belongs to Kant's inventory of objects of the minds can be representations. Yet, if you make the notion of a *Vorstellung* into what might be called an umbrella word which can be used to designate any of those objects but cannot itself designate a unique kind of object called a representation, you escape one problem only to face another. For you cannot account for states of consciousness like sensations and nonexistent objects that have no objects at all.

The notion of an *Anschauung* joins its predecessors for much the same reason. It cannot be defined without circularity in terms of other notions that play a part in Kant's philosophy. And the attempt to define it independently of those notions only serves to make it applicable to a domain of objects of possible but not actualizable intuition.

We have a choice between rendering *Erkenntnis* as "knowledge" or "cognition," one of which is and the other not, a case of judging. This distinction, valid though it is, threatens the more basic Kantian distinction between transcendental and metaphysical knowledge. If you choose to render Kant's notion of *Wirklichkeit* as "actuality" rather than "reality," you succeed in making one part of Kant's theory intelligible only to block accessibility to another part of that theory; namely, the argument of the Postulates, which appears to run against the grain of what Kant says he is doing when he demonstrates the necessary applicability of the categories to all objects of possible experience.

The distinction between *Wille* and *Willkür* raises further difficulties for the understanding of central themes in Kant's moral philosophy. On one rendering, there can be no free action. On another, there is no difference between an elective and a legislative will. And, as we have seen, this is not an isolated occurrence in Kant's philosophical vocabulary. It arises all over again in his aesthetic theory. If we choose to render *Zweckmäßigkeit* as "finality," we make it impossible to distinguish, as Kant repeatedly does, between natural and artistic objects.

All of this constitutes a set of conditions for the possibility of any future translation of Kant's work. But it is more than that. The set of problems and perplexities which has been surveyed briefly here betokens the profound philosophical issues which must be resolved if we are to establish a framework within which translation of Kant is possible at all.

Iowa City, Iowa   MOLTKE S. GRAM
1982

RICHARD E. AQUILA

Is Sensation the Matter of Appearances?

1

It is difficult to know, in translation, how accurately one ought to re-
produce elements of vagueness or ambiguity apparently present in
the original. In addition, of course, disagreement as to precisely
where a text is in fact vague or ambiguous often reflects some prior
difference in its interpretation as a whole. Consider the question
whether, in Kant's view, the "immediate objects" of perception are
subjective entities of some sort. Are they, for example, just our own
perceptions or sensations, somehow spatio-temporally arranged and
projected into a space that we apprehend as outside of ourselves?
Are sensations the "matter" or the "material" of *Erscheinungen?* In some
passages Kant explicitly says that sensation is the matter of perception (*Wahrnehmung*): A167/B209; or of our sensory knowledge: A42/
B59-60, A50/B74.[1] There are also passages which at least *suggest,*
even strongly, that sensation is the matter of *appearances,* and not just
of our perceptions *of* appearances. Translations, as I shall try to show,
tend to convert these suggestions into firm assertions. There in fact
seem to be few, if any, passages which are unequivocal in this respect.
The texts, in short, display much more ambiguity than current translations suggest.

It may well be Kant's view that something that he calls *Empfindung*
is the material of outer appearances. But it is not unreasonable to
suppose that this involves a different *use* of the term from one which

Richard E. Aquila is professor of philosophy, University of Tennessee, Knoxville.

would license the conclusion that the material of appearances is certain sorts of "subjective entities," i.e., *our* "sensations." That use would differ from Kant's own *official* use, and it would, as I shall suggest in section 2, be one which is in fact new with Kant. So long, of course, as this supposition is a reasonable one, the translator needs to exercise more than customary caution in rendering passages unambiguous and in making what seem obvious implications explicit. It may, after all, be precisely Kant's tendency both to depart from and to adhere to his own official usage that *accounts* for the ambiguity in most of the relevant passages. If, of course, Kant explicitly *says* that *Empfindung* is the material of appearances, then, whether we think that he is using the term in accordance with his own official use, or in some other way, we have little choice but to translate it just as we otherwise would; presumably, that is, as "sensation." But we ought, at the same time, to attempt to minimize the number of passages where this is unavoidable.

Now at A167/B208-209, Kant says that *Empfindung* is something *an den Erscheinungen,* and that it is the *Materie der Wahrnehmung.* At B147, one might also note, Kant says that spatio-temporal *objects* are themselves *Wahrnehmungen,* that is, *mit Empfindung begleitete Vorstellungen.* But it is not unreasonable to suppose, as we shall see, that all three of the terms *Empfindung, Vorstellung,* and *Wahrnehmung* have a special use in Kant, in addition to their official Kantian one. In any case, the passage in question seems explicit enough in asserting that sensation is an ingredient in appearances, and not just in our perceptions *of* them. At best there is, with respect to the translation of this passage, only one locus for possible disagreement. This concerns the translation of the preposition *an.* Is Kant indeed saying that sensation is an ingredient *in* appearances? Or is he perhaps only saying that sensation is an element somehow closely *connected* with, or in some sense *attached* to, appearances?

It is worth noting that in this section ("The Anticipations of Perception") Kant speaks nine times of something *in der Erscheinung* or *in den Erscheinungen.* In none of these instances does he explicitly say that *Empfindung* is what is in question. Once he speaks of *etwas,* in a context which seems to *refer* that term to an earlier occurrence of *Empfindung.* But while that is, in some respects, the most natural reading of the passage, it is not in all respects so, as I shall show later. So that passage can't count as one of the "explicit" ones in Kant. In all the other passages in this section, Kant is talking about *das Reale* or *Realität* (which he speaks of several times as what *corresponds* to sensation), or about the intensive magnitude thereof, as what is "in" appearances. He also speaks of sensation as something in (*in*) *Bewusstsein, Wahrnehmung,* and *Erfahrung;* and of "the real" or "reality" in (*in*) *Anschauung, Wahrnehmung,* and *Raum.* So perhaps there is some significance in the fact that the only apparently explicit passage, with respect to the question at hand, avoids the use of *in* altogether for *an.* Does it signal, perhaps, a special use for *Empfindung* (namely, that which "corresponds" to *Empfindung* in the primary sense)? It is, of course, difficult to be sure. But at the very least, I think, a translation ought to indicate the uncertainty surrounding this point. None, to my knowledge, does so.

Consider, similarly, *Prolegomena* (sec. 11, p. 284). Here Kant speaks of *die Materie der Erscheinung, d.i. das, was in ihr Empfindung ist.* Beck translates: "the matter of the phenomenon (that is, the sensation in it)."[2] The same, roughly, with Ellington's recent revision of the Carus translation.[3] Carus himself, though, spoke not of "sensation" but of "the sense element" in phenomena (although he *elsewhere* translates *Empfindung* in the more customary way).[4] Now what Kant literally *says* (to use, admittedly, what may be a meaningless phrase) is that the matter of phenomena is *that which is sensation* in it. Did Kant mean to suggest, then, that *that which is* "sensation" in the *phenomenon* is not quite the same thing as what we call "sensation" as a state of *ourselves,* but at most, perhaps, something that "corresponds" to it? Carus' caution suggests that he may have thought so. (Another apparently explicit passage in the *Prolegomena* [sec. 24, p. 307] says that sensations are what *ausmachen* the *eigentliche Qualität* of appearances. So they "constitute," as the translations have it, the sensory "quality" of appearances, as opposed to their "form": the passage corresponds to the Anticipations of Perception. But "constitute," happily, is as ambiguous as *ausmachen.* In any case, one ought not to suppose that Kant has said that sensations *are* the qualitative or the material aspect of appearances. And earlier in the section in question he had in fact said that sensation "indicates" or "denotes" [*Bezeichnet*] the "real of intuitions," and that it "posits" [*setzt*] an object *corresponding* to it, i.e., to sensation, in space and time.)

In some other passages, the ambiguity in question concerns the reference of pronouns. Consider, e.g., Beck's translation of *Prolegomena* (sec. 26, p. 309): ". . . insofar as the perception contains, besides intuition, sensation . . . it is apparent that the real within appearances must have a degree, so far as it (namely, the sensation) *does not itself occupy any part of space or of time."* Ellington's translation reads the same, except for replacing "namely" with *viz.* within the parentheses. No parenthesis occurs in the original, nor is the word *Empfindung* repeated. Kant simply says that "the real within appearances must have a degree, so far as *it*" does not occupy space or time. The "it" (*sie*) may refer, grammatically, to perception, sensation, or intuition, but only the first two avoid contradiction in the text. Carus chooses "perception." But Ellington and Beck are probably right in choosing "sensation." All three, in any case, introduce a parenthetical phrase giving definiteness to what is indefinite in the text. In so doing, however, both Ellington and Beck imply that Kant has said that the *real within appearance* is sensation, which he does not. Carus avoids this suggestion, one might note, not only by referring the pronoun in question to *Wahrnehmung,* but also by translating *Empfindung* as "sensibility," even though he translates it as "sensation" in Kant's footnote in that very sentence. No one would suppose, of course, that either "perception" or "sensibility" is, on Kant's view, the "real within appearances."

Contrary, then, to what (in notable contrast to Carus) current translations suggest, it is not clear that any of the passages in the *Prolegomena* explicitly asserts that *Empfindung* is the material of appearances.

Before returning to the *Critique of Pure Reason,* incidentally, let me also take the occasion to note a mistranslation of a passage from the *Critique of Judgment.* Bernard reads as follows ("Introduction," sec. VII):

> *Sensation,* again (i.e. external sensation), expresses the merely subjective [element] of our representations of external things, but it is also the proper material (reale) of them (by which something existing is given), just as space is the mere form *a priori* of the possibility of their intuition.[5]

But what Kant himself says is that sensation expresses (*drückt . . . aus*) the subjective element in our representations of external things; then [comma] "but properly [*eigentlich*] the material (or real) [*das Materielle (Reale)*] of them." Thus Kant does not say that sensation *is* the material of external things, but only that it *expresses* it. (Meredith gets this right: *"Sensation . . .* agrees in expressing a merely subjective side of our representations of external things, but one which is properly their matter. . . .")[6]

Let me return, now, to the second of the passages in the Anticipations of Perception chapter which seem to be "explicit" in identifying sensation with the material aspect of appearances. Here (if it makes sense to say so) is a literal translation of the passage:

Apprehension solely by means of sensation occupies only a moment (if, namely, I ignore the succession of many sensations). As something in [*in*] the appearance, the apprehension of which is not a successive synthesis which proceeds from parts to the whole representation, it [*sie*] therefore has no extensive magnitude; the lack of sensation in that moment would represent it as empty, therefore = 0. [A167-8/B209]

Meiklejohn, Max Müller, and Kemp Smith[7] make what appears to be on stylistic and grammatical grounds a reasonable assumption that the "it" which Kant infers, in the second sentence, to lack extensive magnitude is the *sensation* mentioned in the sentence preceding. This they do, one might note, despite the fact that Kant had spoken, in the preceding sentence, of the apprehension of something by *means* of sensation, whereas he now supposedly refers *back,* on this reading, to that very sensation as something which is *what* is apprehended by means of sensation (hence, apparently, by itself!). This they do, in addition, despite the fact that in the immediately succeeding sentence Kant refers to that "in" (*in*) the appearance which *corresponds* to sensation, namely *Realität.* To the latter, in turn, he refers two more times in that paragraph as something which is "in the appearance." In all three of these succeeding sentences, Kant uses *both* the term *Empfindung* and *Realität* (or *das Reale*). But he avoids speaking of the *first* of these as something "in" the appearance. Finally, in the last sentence of the paragraph, Kant repeats the locution *Apprehension . . . vermittelst der blossen Empfindung,* referring, clearly, to *das Reale* as what is apprehended in that way. In any case, the translators' assumption remains reasonable on stylistic grounds, and all three of them therefore *replace* the original *pronoun* with a more definite reference to "sensation." Thus Kemp Smith: "As sensation is that element in the [field of] appearance the apprehension of which does not involve a successive synthesis proceeding from parts to the whole representation, it has no extensive magnitude."

Unfortunately, while the translators' assumption is the most reasonable one on stylistic grounds, it is not the only possible one. As we have already seen, the assumption is unreasonable on *conceptual* grounds, given the rest of the paragraph. In addition, it is not the only *grammatical* possibility. Though it requires, admittedly, a bit of stretching, the pronoun *could* refer to the *Materie* to which Kant had just referred at the end of the preceding paragraph. Then what we would have is this (modifying Kemp Smith's translation):

For it does indeed seem surprising that we should anticipate experience, precisely in that which concerns what is only to be obtained through it, namely, its matter. Yet, none the less, such is actually the case.

Apprehension by means merely of sensation occupies only an instant, if, that is, I do not take into account the succession of different sensations. As something in the appearance, the apprehension of which is not a successive synthesis which proceeds from parts to the whole representation, it [namely, *die Materie*] therefore has no extensive magnitude . . . .

This is possible grammatically. It is also, though a bit awkward, not impossible stylistically. And it is, again, the most reasonable reading *conceptually*. So I don't think a translation should rule it out.

There is, incidentally, at least one other passage in the *Critique* where this sort of stretching of a pronoun's reference seems to occur. Unfortunately, translators haven't agreed on just *what* the pronouns in question refer to. Here is Kemp Smith, somewhat modified:

We know nothing but our mode [*Art*] of perceiving [things] — a mode which is peculiar to us, and not necessarily shared in by every being, though, certainly, by every human being. With this alone have we any concern. Space and time are its pure forms, and sensation in general its matter. The former alone can we know *a priori*, that is, prior to all actual perception; and it [Kemp Smith: such knowledge; Meiklejohn: such cognition; Müller: space and time] is therefore called pure intuition. The latter is that in our knowledge [neuter] which leads to our calling it [feminine, nonetheless Müller: our knowledge] *a posteriori* knowledge, that is, empirical intuition. [A42/B59-60]

Though no translator takes it this way, the only reading which is both grammatically possible and accurate to content takes the pronouns in question to refer back to our "mode [*Art*] of perceiving." With respect to the forms of space and time, that is, our "mode of perceiving" is a pure intuition; with respect to the presence of sensation in it, an empirical intuition. Admittedly, the reference back to the noun in question is a rather long one. So one might conclude that this couldn't be the reference Kant had in mind. One might also take it, though, simply as evidence that Kant occasionally employs a rather long, somewhat awkward pronominal reference.

Now let me turn, finally, to Kant's first introduction of the sensation/matter distinction. After defining *Empfindung* as the effect (*Wirkung*) of an object, *qua* effect (*sofern wir von demselben affiziert werden*) on our representative faculty, and *Erscheinung* as *der unbestimmte Gegenstand* of an intuition by means of sensation (an empirical intuition), Kant says that the *Materie* of appearance is that in (*in*) the appearance which corresponds (*Korrespondiert*) to sensation (A19-20/B34). By itself, of course, this locution does not rule out the possibility that sensation also *is* the matter of an appearance. Consider, for example, the claim that the rain which falls from the clouds is what "corresponds" to the material of our lakes and streams. That same rain also *is* the material of those watery bodies. But we might also say that it merely "corresponds" to that material. We would do so, presumably, in order to indicate the difference between the rain's status *qua* falling from clouds, and its status *qua* lake and stream material. Thus, John Watson:

> The sensations are in *content* the same as before, but this content is now *formed*. Now, as "matter" and "form" are correlative, we cannot call the sensations *before* they are ordered the "matter" of the object; what we must say is, that in the object they *become* "matter." Hence, in the perceived object the "matter" *corresponds* to what prior to this object was pure sensation.

We don't have to look as far back as Watson, of course, to find this sort of extreme subjectivism ascribed to Kant. Consider T. E. Wilkerson's recent "commentary for students" of the *Critique*. Here is what he says about the claim the space is the form of intuition for Kant: "We know that 'intuition' [i.e., empirical intuition] means 'sense impression'. . . . Presumably a 'form' is some principle of arrangement, a rule of organization or relation between things. If we translate the reference to forms and intuitions into more familiar terms, then Kant's slogan becomes the claim that experiences are spatially and temporally related."[9] In this passage, of course, Wilkerson, at the very least, confuses intuition with sensation. In any case, the view he ascribes to Kant is that the immediate objects of sensory awareness are just our own sensations, spatially organized. He concludes, therefore, that "Transcendental idealism is essentially a mixture of certain rationalist doctrines and Berkeleian idealism. . . ."[10] Jonathan Bennett, on the other hand, takes pain to distinguish Kant's idealism from Berkeley's. But he does not dispute the claim that, for Kant, the immediate objects of sensory awareness are mental entities. The point he makes is simply that, for Kant, it is not literally that case that a material object literally is a *collection* of such entities. It is, rather, a "logical construction" out of them.[11]

But now consider Kant's next claims. Here is a "literal" translation:

> . . . that which determines that the manifold of appearance can be ordered in certain relations, I call the *form* of appearance. Since that in which alone sensations can be ordered, and placed in a certain form, cannot in turn be itself sensation, while the matter of all appearance is given only a posteriori, its

form must lie ready for them a priori in the mind, and therefore allow of being
considered apart from all sensation.

Grammatically, it isn't perfectly clear what the "them" in question
refers to ("its form must lie ready for *them* a priori in the mind").
Kemp Smith translates: "its form must lie ready for the sensations a
priori in the mind." Both Müller and Meiklejohn leave the pronoun
as it stands, without substituting a noun for it. But both of them do
change Kant's singular "appearance" to the plural. Thus, presumably,
they take the reference to be to appearances, not sensations.

Kant himself, incidentally, does not hesitate, on occasion, to con-
nect a plural pronoun with an original singular noun. Thus A92/
B125: "And this is the case with appearance [*Erscheinung*], with respect
to that in them [*an ihnen*] which belongs to sensation." Here, Kemp
Smith notes that he is, with Grillo, correcting Kant's original singular
to plural. Both Meiklejohn and Müller make the corresponding
change in English. But there is of course no need for this correction.
It is not impossible to read the sentence just as I translated it. There
is a similar passage at A123: ". . . insofar as it, with respect to all the
manifold of appearance, aims at nothing beyond the necessary unity
in the synthesis *derselben.*" Kemp Smith translates "In so far as it aims
at nothing but necessary unity in the synthesis of what is manifold in
appearance . . . ," although that, of course, would have required *desselben,* and not *derselben* in the original. Müller proceeds in roughly
the same way. But the most reasonable assumption, it seems to me,
is that Kant is referring to the synthesis of *appearances,* even though
the noun in question appeared originally only in the singular:
". . . with respect to all the manifold of appearance, aims at nothing
beyond the necessary unity in *their* synthesis." Perhaps the most
noteworthy passage of this sort is one which might also appear to be
explicit in identifying sensations as the material of appearances:

> For in order that certain sensations be referred to something outside me (that
> is, to something in another region of space from that in which I find myself),
> and similarly in order that I may be able to represent them as outside and
> alongside one another . . . the representation of space must be presupposed.
> [A23/B38]

Both Kemp Smith and Hans Vaihinger take the "them" to refer back
to the sensations of which Kant speaks in the first clause.[12] Abstractly
considered, this is of course the most reasonable move stylistically.
But it is not the only possible one. For it is not impossible to suppose

that the term in fact refers to the "something" (*etwas*) to which those sensations are originally said to be *referred*. Once we take note of some *other* passages in which Kant divides the reference of an originally singular noun, by means of a subsequent plural in the pronoun, there is no reason to suppose that this is not in fact the correct reading, or even to suppose that Kant is being particularly careless in this passage.

The moral with respect to A20/B34, of course, is that there is no reason for supposing that Kant is claiming, in that passage, that the form *of appearances* is a form with respect to which sensations provide the material. Undeniably, Kant does speak in that passage of a form in which sensations are ordered. And he also does *infer* from the fact that this form cannot itself be derived from sensation, that a *corresponding* form (of appearances) must in some sense "lie ready" for *something* in the mind. Both Müller and Meiklejohn suppose, as I have noted, that the something is *appearances*. And they go, in fact, so far as to change Kant's original "appearance" to the plural in order to indicate this fact. I suspect that they are right, though there is, so far as I can see, no need to make the change in question to legitimize the reading. In any case, the passage is certainly compatible, despite Kemp Smith's translation, with the supposition the sensation at most *corresponds* to the material of appearances.

So much, then, for my attempt to show that the relevant texts are much less definite, and much more ambiguous, than translations have tended to show. Let me turn now to some speculation concerning the *sources* of this ambiguity in Kant.

2

There is reason in Kant's thought both for and against a use of the term *Empfindung* to stand for an object of sense perception (or for an aspect *of* the objects of sense perception). There is reason, that is, both for and against Kant's use of the term to stand for the "sensible qualities" of objects, apart from their spatial form. To do so, of course, would be to use a single term to stand both for some aspect of a state of sensory awareness and also for some aspect of the *object* of such a state.

In general there would have been nothing odd, in the philosophical or even in the more everyday usage of Kant's time, in employing the same term to stand both for the act whereby some object is presented to the consciousness and the *object* thereby presented. Thus Adelung (1793-1801) distinguishes two main uses of the term *Vorstellung* (which for Kant, is the genus of which *Empfindung* is a species): (1) *Die Handlung des vorstellens;* (2) *Was vorgestellt wird.*[13] One of the more everyday instances of the distinction was, of course, that between the presentation of a stage play and the *play* thereby presented. But Adelung also offers, with respect to the second, "objective" use, "in a narrower and proper sense the image which one frames of a thing in one's thoughts (*das Bild, welches man sich, von einer Sache in Gedanken macht*), in a wider sense, however, any concept of a thing, or idea (ein jeder Begriff von einer Sache, die Idee)." Campe (1811) draws the same distinction between the presenting of something and the thing presented. But, unlike Adelung, he does not specifically single out the notion of *Bild* in connection with the second of these uses.[14] Naturally, philosophical usage at this time had an influence on more general usage. As the brothers Grimm observed, however, the usage of the term which eventually came to dominate, namely that wherein the "verbal meaning" tended to disappear, first achieved its predominance in the eighteenth century, and *"then* was taken over, with more precise definition, into the technical language of philosophy (*die in schärferer Bestimmung dann in die technische Sprache der Philosophie übernommen wird*)."[15] In any case, while Adelung characterizes *Empfindung* as a species of *Vorstellung,* in the third of three definitions listed for that term, presentation through the *senses* is not included as one of the instances lending itself to an "objective" as opposed to a primarily verbal use of the latter term. He includes only the "images" of objects in *thought,* together with concepts or "ideas." Like Kant too, one might note, Adelung characterizes the "representative" character of sensation by reference to the fact that it is an *effect* brought about by some object within the perceiver.

It is at this point that philosophical *theory,* and perhaps some careless psychology, legitimizes a dual use of *Empfindung,* paralleling that of *Vorstellung* but never, like the latter, achieving a genuinely "definitional" status. Sensations, that is, are regarded, by some philosophers at least, not only as the internal effects whereby we become *aware* of objects of sensation, but also as themselves *among* the proper objects of sensation. Thus Descartes, as is well known, classifies "light and colour, sounds, odours, tastes, heat, hardness, and all other tactile qualities" as sensations.[16] One is inclined, of course, to regard all these as material objects or qualities, or at least to *resemble* such objects or qualities. But this would be a mistake, in Descartes' view. Compare, similarly, the following passage from Tetens' *Philosophische Versuche.* Sensation, Tetens says, is "that which we take not so much for a quality (*Beschaffenheit*) of ourselves, as rather for a copy (*Abbildung*) of an object which we believe that we sense *through* it."[17] Thus whether or not the sensations in question are in fact copies of an external object, they are *themselves* among the proper objects of sensory awareness. For if they were not, then they could not be what we tend to *take* to be copies of external objects.

Notice one difference between the duality legitimized by common usage, with respect to the term *Vorstellung,* and that assumed by some philosophers to attach to *Empfindung.* Philosophers who use the latter term to stand not only for an aspect of perceptual awareness, but also for such objects as (perceived) colors, sounds, etc., tend to make the following assumption. They assume, namely, that the term thus employed stands, in both instances, *for the very same thing.* In their view, that is, perceived colors and sounds just *are* certain effects within the perceiver. It is important to be clear, however, that this assumption is by no means implied in the commonly recognized duality of the term *Vorstellung.* That usage legitimizes application of the term to at least certain sorts of presented, or presentable, *objects.* But it does not suggest that those objects are themselves *the same thing as* the presentation of them, or the same thing as some *aspect* of that presentation. We are dealing, in this case, with the dual use of a single *term.* But there is no need to assume that this usage rests, in turn, on a dual role played by some single *entity.*

This difference may seem to be blurred by Adelung's examples. As examples of *Vorstellungen* in the "objective" sense, he offers *Begriff* and *Idee.* These, it would seem, are not so much represented *objects* as they are our representations *of* objects, or some aspect of that representation. Or if they *are* represented objects, then they are objects which are somehow *identical* with the representation of them, or with some aspect of that representation. In philosophical writing, however, the term "concept" or "idea" is very often used precisely to stand for some object which is presented to the mind, as *distinguished* from the presentation of it. Nor do I intend, in saying this, merely to indicate the possibility of construing these terms *Platonistically.* Consider, for example, the distinction as Descartes drew it.

> In this term *idea* there is here something equivocal, for it may either be taken materially, as an act of my understanding, and in this sense it cannot be said to be more perfect than I; or it may be taken objectively, as the thing which is represented by this act, which, although we do not suppose it to exist outside of my understanding, may none the less, be more perfect than I, because of its essence.[18]

My idea of infinite perfection, to take Descartes' example, is either my *thoughts* about infinite perfection (or some quality of those thoughts), or it is infinite perfection *itself*. But if the latter, Descartes says, then only on the *proviso* that the idea in question is infinite perfection *as it exists in my understanding*. There are two things that Descartes might mean by this *proviso*. (1) The (objective) idea of infinite perfection may be infinite perfection considered merely *as an intentional object*. By this I don't mean that one's (material) idea of infinite perfection involves a relation to some entity which *is* the (intentional) object in question. I mean, rather, to be using the term more in Brentano's sense. In this sense, "intentional objects" are merely "linguistic correlates" of (material) ideas:

> I allowed myself the term 'immanent object', in order to say not that the object exists, but that it *is* an object whether or not there is anything that corresponds to it. Its *being* an object, however, is merely the linguistic correlate of the person experiencing *having* it as object, i.e., his thinking of it in his experience.[19]

(2) The (objective) idea of infinite perfection might be construed more ontologically in terms of the Scholastic notion of the attributes or forms or natures or essences of things somehow being "received into" the cognitive faculties of the knower. It is, of course, difficult to know how literally to take the Scholastic notion of reception "within" the knower. At the very least, it seems to imply that a (material) idea involves some actual cognitive *relation* with something, namely with the form or nature or essence of some (possible) object. It is well known that Descartes rejected a Scholastic account of sense perception (in terms of the "reception" of "sensible form"). But it has been argued, rather convincingly I think, that Descartes did not depart very far from the Scholastic approach to intellection or to intellectual "ideas."[20] (Certainly, the argument for the existence of God, which the distinction in question was intended to support, requires an ontological approach.) In any case, neither interpretation requires literally *identifying* an idea "objectively" considered with one "materially" considered. In both cases we are dealing with a relation between act and object. It is important to observe, however, that on the intentional object approach, one might nonetheless regard an (objective) idea as something which does not exist outside of, or apart from, the material idea intending it. This would be the sense in which an intentional object is not, at least *qua* intentional object, anything apart from the awareness of it. But that of course is not to say the object is some

entity which is either identical with the awareness of it or with some aspect of that awareness. For it is not something which, in itself, is regarded as an entity at all. To talk about it is just to talk about the fact that certain sorts of mental activities are possible. But that does not make it, literally, an aspect of mental activity.

On the Scholastic theory, the distinction just drawn with respect to intellection applies to sensation as well. We could distinguish, in other words, between a "sensation," or "sensory idea" construed as the "reception" of the sensible form of some (possible) object; and sensation, or sensory ideas, construed as the sensible forms thus received. This, of course, would involve employing Cartesian terminology in a Scholastic framework. There is no *a priori* reason against doing so. One often-noted danger is that of confusing "sensory ideas" in the sense of *sensation* and in the sense of *intellectual* ideas of the possible objects of sensation. (Descartes himself falls prey to this danger on more than one occasion. His suggestion that sensations are "confused" forms of intellection seems to rest on the error, for example.)[21] In any case, Kant is as emphatic as Descartes in rejecting the notion of a reception, within the perceiver, of the sensible forms of objects. For both philosophers, rather, sensation, as such, is at most an *effect* from an external object, not a cognitive relation with it:

> *Sensuality* is the *receptivity* of a subject by which it is possible for the subject's own representative state to be affected in a definite way by the presence of . . . things which cannot by their own quality enter into the senses of that subject (*quae in sensus ipsius per qualitatem suam incurrere non possunt*).[22]

At this point, we need to distinguish two views about the role of sensation in perception. Since sensation by itself, in this view, is not the presentation of anything to consciousness (or at best the presentation of a way in which the subject is affected), the sensory presentation of *spatial forms* will need to involve some ingredient in addition to the mere sensation involved. There are two possibilities. (1) The additional ingredient involves the presence of a presentative state in *addition* to the sensation involved, and together with it forms a complex state. (2) The additional ingredient, together with the sensation involved, forms a single presentative state, but not one which is a complex of two *distinct* presentative states. There is some reason to think that the first of these alternatives is that of Descartes: spatial form is represented only by intellectual "ideas"; these, therefore, must be *added* to mere sensation in order to provide the sensory presentation of, as opposed to a pure thought about, some spatial expanse. For Kant, on the other hand, the presentation of spatial form in sense perception is precisely *by means of* the sensation involved in it. It is by means of that sensation, that is, insofar as it exhibits the appropriate cognitive "form." It is precisely this view, one might in fact suggest, that accounts not only for Kant's rejection, with Descartes, of the Scholastic account of sensation, but also for the conclusion, which Descartes does not share, that the only objects of genuine cognitive relations are "appearances":

> I can only know what is contained in the object in itself if it is present and given to me. It is indeed even then incomprehensible how the intuition of a present thing should make me know this thing as it is in itself, as its properties cannot migrate into my faculty of representation (*da ihre Eigenschaften nicht in meine Vorstellungskraft hinüberwandern können*) . . . .[23]

Representational quality for Kant is not some sort of basic cognitive *relation*. Rather, it is a function of the internal "form" of a state (and of the relation between that state and *other* possible states). Therefore, Kant seems to conclude, the immediate objects of representation are, as such, *intentional objects,* and in that sense, mere "appearances."[24]

There obviously is, as we have seen, a tendency for Kant to regard the immediate objects of sensory presentation as sensations organized in spatial forms. But as we have also seen, some of the passages that appear to support this supposition at most imply that the sensory *presentation* of spatial forms are sensations that are organized in certain "forms," though not necessarily spatial ones. "Form," in this case, is whatever minimal conditions must be exhibited by a sensory state, over and above a certain standard sort of causal relation (i.e., involving sense organs) with some object, in order for that state to constitute a cognitively relevant presentation of spatial form. This is at most what is implied in the passage that we examined from the beginning of the Aesthetic. And it is also all that is implied in Kant's claims that sensation is the "matter" of perception (*Wahrnehmung*): A167/209; or of our sensory knowledge (*Erkenntnis*): A50/B74. Similarly for the following passage from the Inaugural Dissertation:

> In a representation of the sense there is first of all something which you might call the *matter,* namely the *sensation,* and there is also something which can be called the *form,* namely the *species* of the sensibles which arises according as the various things which affect the senses are coordinated by a certain natural law of the mind . . . . For objects do not strike the senses in virtue of their form or *species.* So, for the various things in an object which affect the sense to coalesce into some representational whole there is needed an internal principle in the mind by which those various things may be clothed with a certain *species* in accordance with stable and innate laws.[25]

Kant's talk about sensations "coalescing" into some "representational whole" may suggest the arrangement of some material into spatial forms. But there is no reason to suppose this is Kant's point. He may simply be saying, rather, that the manifold of affection-relations in which the subject may happen to stand to something outside of itself never amounts, as such, to the presentation of an object. In addition, there needs to be a certain character *within the effected state*. Not *any* set of effects on a subject's sense organs constitutes a cognitively *relevant* effect. Any set of such effects which would constitute, together, a cognitively relevant state must exhibit, as a whole, a special sort of cognitively relevant *feature;* a feature, that is, over and above the fact that the state is, or is composed of parts which are, generated in a certain way. This feature Kant calls the intuitional "form" of the state.

Suppose, then, that this is Kant's view. If it is, then we can conclude that there both is and is not a sense in which "sensation," on Kant's view, provides the material of appearances. Suppose we mean by "sensation" a certain sort of internal state, or aspect of such a state. This, of course, is part of Kant's own official definition of the term. It was also general standard philosophical usage since Descartes. Now sensation, in this sense, is in Kant's view an ingredient in our sensory representation of spatial forms. It is that aspect of such representation which accounts for it being a *seeing* of such forms, for example, as opposed to merely imagining them in a kind of "pure intuition."[26] It is that aspect, in other words, which accounts for the presentation of a spatial expanse filled with yellow rather than, say, red. But in that case, we can conclude, the sensations which are ingredient in a total sensory presentation represent, not simply some internal effect within us, but also a certain aspect of the appearances which present themselves *to* us, for example, their color.

It is clear that Kant often avails himself of the terminological license whereby the term *Vorstellung,* and its relatives, apply both to our being presented with some object and also to the object thus presented (at least *qua* "intentional object"). Thus at B147, Kant says that spatio-temporal objects are themselves *Wahrnehmungen.* In that passage, too, and also at A30/B45, he says that such objects are mere *Vorstellung,* and its relatives, apply both to our being presented with some object and also to the object thus presented (at least *qua* "intentional object"). Thus at B147, Kant says that spatio-temporal objects are themselves *Wahrnehmungen.* In that passage, too, and also at A30/B45, he says that such objects are mere *Vorstellungen.* And in a number of places (e.g., A163/B204, B207, A168/B209) he says that they are *Anschauungen*. Some commentators assume, of course, that Kant means that the objects in question are just our own mental states, or collections of such states, or some sort of "logical construction" out of them; at the very least, they assume, it is our own mental states which are the immediate objects of perception on Kant's view. As I have pointed out, however, it is perfectly appropriate, both in philosophical literature and in ordinary language, to use the term *Vorstellung* to stand for the *object* of a presentative state without making any such assumption. In order to account for the sorts of usage in question, we need only assume, then, that Kant was prepared to broaden customary usage beyond the case of imagination and thought, to the point of including sense perception.

Unlike Descartes, it would have been perfectly natural for Kant to extend customary usage in this way. In Descartes' view what is properly "presentative" about sensory awareness seems to be wholly due to the *intellectual* ideas connected with sensation. Apart from that, all that one is presented with in sensation are just one's own subjective states. But in Kant's view, it is precisely through the *vehicle* of sensations that sensory presentation is constituted. Hence sensory presentation (though not mere "sensation") is always, as such, object-directed (at least, that is toward an "intentional object"). It always involves what Descartes would call the "objective presence" of some object; it is not merely *intellectual* "ideas" of which alone this can strictly be said. So it is natural for Kant to extend the ordinary license concerning the term *Vorstellung* to include the sensory presentation of spatial forms. And given this, it is also natural to extend the use of various other terms, such as *Wahrnehmung* and *Anschauung*. It was, of course, customary to regard the latter, and *Empfindung* as well, as forms of *Vorstellung*. What requires an extension of customary usage (apart, of course, from a Cartesian or a Berkeleian view of sensation) was the application of the terms in question to the corresponding *objects*. This extension, as I have tried to show, should carry no Berkeleian or Cartesian implication at all. For it does not imply that the object of the corresponding subjective states is identical with such states themselves, or with some aspect of such states. As one might note, after all, Kant also speaks of Space and Time as *Anschauungen* and as *Vorstellungen* (cf. A24/B38, A31/B46, B147, 160, 207). Surely he does not mean that space and time are mental states, or aspects of them. They are, rather, (intentional) *objects* of such states (albeit objects of a universal pervasiveness), and exist only *as* such objects. (I mean, of course, to include *possible* states here: space and time, and all "appearances," are real insofar as they are *possible* [intentional] objects.)

Given this much, then, we can also see that it would be natural for Kant to extend his use of the term *Empfindung*. For insofar as appearances, *qua* intentional objects of sense presentation, contain an aspect which corresponds to the presence of sensation in a sensory state, it would not be inappropriate to extend the term *Empfindung* to signify this aspect. After all, the element of sensation in our sense presentations is, in an important sense, the *Vorstellung* of that aspect of appearances. But it should also be clear why Kant would be hesitant about adopting this sort of terminology. First, on Kant's view, sensations constitute the presentation of the "material" aspect of appearances only insofar as they are ingredient in *intuitions*. Hence, unlike intuitions, they are not *as such* representations of the material aspect of appearances. Second, while it was customary, as we have seen, to apply the term *Vorstellung* both to presentative states (or certain aspects of them) and to the objects of those states (at least *qua* presented or presentable), it was not part of generally established usage to do this in the case of *Empfindung*. Rather, the latter usage would have been generally appropriate only if one held a very un-Kantian view, namely, that certain entities (or states) which are internal modifications of ourselves are *also* among the proper objects of sense perception. That philosophical view is especially difficult to hold when sensations are regarded as intrinsic to the sensory presentation of objects. But some philosophers, as we have seen, have a tendency to regard sensory presentation as wholly a function of intellectual ideas somehow related *to* sensations. In an important sense, this gives sensations a peculiar role extrinsic to the function of sensory presentation proper. Given that, some philosophers apparently find it tempting to regard them as functioning among the objects *of* sensory presentation. But on Kant's view, sensations do not float free of sensory presentation in this way.

To conclude, then, (1) considerations internal to Kant's thought, and in fact constituting what he himself regarded as among his most important insights, lead to an extension of the term *Empfindung* to the material aspect of appearances. This extension, furthermore, given the relevant philosophical viewpoint, would not have constituted an intolerable departure from everyday usage, and certainly not from philosophical usage. In any case, it would be consistent with the Kantian extension of other, related terms. (2) On the other hand, extension of the term in this case was bound to be misleading in a way that the other instances are not. The conflict between these two considerations explains, I would suggest, much of the ambiguity in Kant's text. Unfortunately, as I have also tried to show, much of the ambiguity fails to reveal itself in translation.

NOTES

1 Page references to the *Critique of Pure Reason* appear in standard form in the text. References to the *Prolegomena* appeal in the text by section number and page number (from vol. 4 of the *Akademie* edition).

2 *Prolegomena*, tr. Lewis White Beck (Indianapolis: Bobbs-Merrill, 1950).

3 *Prolegomena*, tr. James W. Ellington (Indianapolis: Hackett, 1977).

4 *Prolegomena*, tr. Paul Carus (Chicago: Open Court, 1902).

5 *Critique of Judgement*, tr. J. H. Bernard (New York: Hafner, 1951). Original ed., pp. xlii-xliii (*Akademie*, vol. 5, p. 189).

6 *Critique of Judgement*, tr. J. C. Meredith (Oxford: Clarendon Press, 1952). Elsewhere in this work Kant refers to sensation as the matter, or the material element, or the "real" element of *Anschauung, Vorstellung, Wahrnehmung,* and of our *Vorstellungszustand:* pp. xlv, 39-40, 153, 157, 205 (*Akademie*, pp. 190, 224, 291, 294, 321).

7 J. M. D. Meiklejohn translation originally published 1855; reprint (London: Bell, 1924). Max Müller original (1881) reprint (Garden City: Doubleday Anchor, 1966). Norman Kemp Smith original (1929) reprint (New York: St. Martin's, 1965).

8 John Watson, *The Philosophy of Kant Explained* (Glasgow: James Maclehose, 1980), p. 76.

9 T. E. Wilkerson, *Kant's Critique of Pure Reason: A Commentary for Students* (Oxford: Clarendon Press, 1976), p. 26.

10 Ibid., p. 27.

11 Jonathan Bennett, *Kant's Analytic* (Cambridge: Cambridge University Press, 1966), pp. 127-29.

12 Hans Vaihinger, *Commentar zu Kant's Kritik der reinen Vernunft,* vol. 2 (Stuttgart: Union Deutsche Verlagsgesellschaft, 1892), pp. 69 ff., p. 165. Norman Kemp Smith, *A Commentary to Kant's "Critique of Pure Reason"* (New York: Humanities Press, 1962; repr. of 2nd ed. of 1923), pp. 85 ff., p. 101.

13   Johann Christoph Adelung, *Grammatisch-Kritisches Wörterbuch der Hochdeutschen Mundart* (Leipzig: Johann Gottlob Immanuel Breitkopf, 1793-1801).

14   Joachim Heinrich Campe, *Wörterbuch der deutschen Sprache* (Braunschweig: in der Schulbuchhandlung, 1811).

15   Jacob and Wilhelm Grimm, *Deutsches Wörterbuch,* vol. 12, pt. 2 (Leipzig: S. Herzel, 1852), p. 1688.

16   Descartes, *Principles of Philosophy,* 1, p. 48 (cf. 66, 68, 70): *The Philosophical Works of Descartes,* tr. Elizabeth S. Haldane and G. R. T. Ross (Cambridge: Cambridge University Press, 1970), vol. 1, pp. 238 ff.

17   Johann Nicolaus Tetens, *Philosophische Versuche über die menschliche Natur und ihre Entwicklung,* vol. 1, p. 214 (Berlin: Kant-Gesellschaft, 1913; reprint of 1775 edition).

18   Descartes, p. 138 ("Preface" to *Meditations*).

19   Franz Brentano, *The True and the Evident,* ed. Oskar Kraus, tr., Roderick Chisholm (New York: Humanities Press, 1966), p. 78.

20   Cf. John W. Yolton, "Ideas and Knowledge in Seventeenth-Century Philosophy," *Journal of the History of Philosophy,* 13 (April 1975), pp. 147 ff; Brian E. O'Neil, *Epistemological Direct Realism in Descartes' Philosophy* (Albuquerque: University of New Mexico Press, 1974), ch. 3; Thomas A. Lennon, "The Inherence Pattern and Descartes' Ideas," *Journal of the History of Philosophy,* 12 (January 1974), pp. 43-52; Richard E. Aquila, *Intentionality: A Study of Mental Acts* (University Park: Pennsylvania State University Press, 1977), ch. 1.

21   Descartes, pp. 237, 247 (*Principles,* 1, pp. 46, 66).

22   Kant, "Inaugural Dissertation," tr. (slightly modified), G. B. Kerferd, in G. B. Kerferd and D. E. Walford, *Kant: Selected Pre-Critical Writings* (New York: Barnes & Noble, 1968), sec. 2, p. 3.

23   Kant, *Prolegomena* (Beck translation), sec. 9 (*Ak.* 4, p. 282).

24   See my "Things in Themselves and Appearances: Intentionality and Reality in Kant," *Archiv für Geschichte der Philosophie,* 61 (1979), and "Intentional Objects and Kantian Appearances," forthcoming, *Philosophical Topics.*

25   Kant, "Dissertation," sec. 2, p. 4 (translation slightly modified).

26   On "pure intuition" as a kind of "imagination," cf. A224/B271, A713/B741.

ROLF GEORGE

Vorstellung and *Erkenntnis* in Kant

The two terms I shall discuss offer difficulties that are due not to the translation of German into English, but to the difficulty of bringing eighteenth-century philosophical concepts into the twentieth. I therefore need not always use the German words to make my point, and will often simply speak of "representation" and "cognition."

I will use as my text the well-known passage C.P.R. A320/B376 f., which contains Kant's polemic against the misuse of the term "idea." Kant here provides us with an inventory of mental occurrences by way of a bifurcating classificatory scheme. The genus, he says, is *representation*. Representations divide into two kinds, conscious and unconscious. A conscious representation is termed *perceptio* (I use the Latin term to avoid confusion with the English translation of *Wahrnehmung*). The other prong of the fork, representing unconscious representations, remains nameless. *Perceptiones* are in turn divided into those that "relate merely to the subject as the modifications of its state," namely *sensations,* and, on the other prong, *cognitions,* that is, *perceptiones* with objects. The scheme continues by dividing cognitions into intuitions and concepts, and then considers the division of concepts. I am not here concerned with this later part and will deal only with the first and third nodes.

Kant owes us a definition of "representation." Indeed, he states two reasons, in rather remote places, why none can be given. He claims, for one thing, that one cannot define "representation" because "what a representation is can only be defined through other representations."[1] This is no more cogent than would be a claim to the

Rolf George is professor of philosophy, University of Waterloo, Waterloo, Ontario, Canada.

effect that one cannot define "word," because to do so would require other words.

More intriguing is the reason he gives in one of the logic lectures: "'Representation,'" he says there, "is the first and most general concept and cannot be defined."[2] It is not clear what he meant by this. Two interpretations seem possible. He may have wanted to make the straightforward and sensible point that "representation" is the first and most general concept in logic, and remains undefined *in this context,* much as, for instance, "symbol" remains undefined in the usual description of logical axiom systems. It would take a mind unusually obsessed with classification to attempt, unsuccessfully one may suppose, a Porphyrian tree that begins with "being" and works its way down through animals, vegetables, and minerals, to arrive eventually at a node for "symbol." When Kant said to his students that "representation" is the most general concept and cannot be defined, he could conceivably have meant that it is the most general concept *in this discipline.*

But it is not likely. He did, after all, say that the concept *cannot* be defined, not that it remains undefined in this context, or that he chose not to define it. Claims of undefinability tended to be absolute. It is overwhelmingly likely, rather, that Kant thought "representation" to be really and truly the highest genus, and that it cannot be defined, much as Aristotle thought that "being," the highest genus, cannot be defined. This is not an absurd claim. If Kant's theoretical philosophy is viewed as a constructional system, then "representation" must denote the ground elements, which cannot be defined in the system. And presumably there is no logical environment in which they *can* be defined. This view of the matter was advanced, for example, by Carl Leonhard Reinhold.[3]

But, despite Kant's disinclination to define, we can say a few things about the Kantian sense of "representation." We can tell from the division of sensations into conscious and unconscious that to have a representation does not imply consciousness of it. This is a point directed against Locke, and represents a feature common to German school philosophy since Leibniz. The next division shows that representations need not have objects. Kant here allows for representations that do not represent. Under the circumstances the choice of the word *Vorstellung* seems odd and calls for an explanation.

Gottsched, of the Wolffian school in the second generation after Leibniz, makes the following point: "The soul represents inwardly those bodies which affect its sensory organs. . . . But the things which affect our senses are all bodies, and these in turn are parts of the world. Hence the soul in all its sensations represents the world. . . . Since we know for certain that the soul has the ability to represent, and since, being a simple thing, it cannot have more than one power, it must be possible to explain all other occurrences in the soul on the basis of this power."[4]

This view, namely, that every mental state refers to something, derives directly from Leibniz, who held not only that every state of the world is mirrored in the soul, but also that every state of the soul mirrors something in the world.[5]

Even before Kant this view was criticized by Crusius, Tetens, and Feder.[6] Kant himself took direct aim at this view in a reflection: "Leibniz takes all sensations (that stem from) certain objects for cognitions of them. But beings who are not the cause of the object through their representations must in the first instance be affected in a certain way so that they can arrive at a cognition of the object's presence. Hence sensation must be the condition of outer representation but not identical with it. . . . Hence cognition is objective, sensation subjective."[7]

Kant here makes a distinction between two relations, namely the relation between a mental state and its cause, and the relation between such a state and its object (if it has an object). The charge against Leibniz is that he confounded the two. A consequence of this confusion is just the view of Wolff and Gottsched: since cause and object are identified, and since every mental state has a cause (as they assumed), it follows that every mental state has an object. But this runs counter not only to the classificatory scheme in our passage, but to the very fabric of the *Critique of Pure Reason*.

When Wolff introduced the term *Vorstellung* into the German philosophical vocabulary as the most general term denoting mental occurrences, he associated with it a certain doctrine: he really thought that every mental state represented something. As it turned out, the word continued to be used as the most general mental term, but the reason for using just this word with its misleading associations was lost when it was no longer assumed that every mental state makes reference to something "in the world." Kant, too, used it in a sense that does not presume representations to have objects: as our text indicates, some representations, i.e., sensations, do not represent anything.

Kant did not assume, however, that there could be an object before the mind only if a referring representation is present. He indicates another sense of "object" in the following passage: "One can indeed call anything, and even any representation, insofar as one is conscious of it, an object. But what this word means in the case of appearances, not insofar as they are, as representations, themselves objects, but insofar as they refer to an object is a subject of deeper enquiry."[8]

I believe that Kant here uses the term "object" (*Objekt*) in the sense of Brentano, a sense that seeks to put distance between the self and its states, so that a sensation, for example, is envisaged as an object of awareness to the self. But Kant was not interested in pursuing this point and immediately sets it aside. He is well aware that one can think of a sensation as *being* an object, even though it is false that it *has* an object. He is concerned almost exclusively with an inquiry into the circumstances under which representations, as tokens or images, come to refer to other things. *This* is the "subject of deeper enquiry" and brings me to the second and more important part of my discussion.

The problems that the choice of the word *Vorstellung* may have caused are as nothing compared with the disastrous misunderstandings occasioned by the word *Erkenntnis*. It is now widely acknowledged that the common English translation of this term as "knowledge" is inaccurate; "cognition" is a far better choice. But as a translation of current German, "knowledge" is good enough. Here, too, the problem lies with understanding the Kantian, and eighteenth century, use of the term.

Johann Christoph Adelung's dictionary of 1793 lists altogether ten senses for *erkennen,* two of which are of interest to us. The first of these requires the direct object construction; in this sense the word means "to represent a thing to oneself, whether we represent it to ourselves clearly or obscurely, distinctly or indistinctly; in this, its widest, meaning, it is very common with recent philosophers."[9]

The second sense of interest to us demands a dependent clause introduced by *dass* or *ob*. Adelung thinks that this use is confined for the most part to the German Bible and the biblical way of writing. In this sense the word may be translated as "to come to know," or "to know." It seems that this second sense of *erkennen* has become very much more common during the nineteenth and twentieth centuries. For example, Adelung does not allow, or even mention, the nominalization *Erkenntnis* in connection with this second sense, but only with the first. By contrast, *Erkenntnis, dass* . . . is now common, whereas *Erkenntnis des/der* (followed by a noun in the genitive) works only for certain lofty subjects, as in *Erkenntnis der Wahrheit, Erkenntnis Gottes,* etc., but not for trees or ships. Thus, while one can say *Ich kann das Schiff gut erkennen* (I can easily discern or make out the ship), this accomplishment may no longer be described as a case of *Erkenntnis.* It follows that the noun, in its current use, may reasonably be translated as "knowledge" and that it no longer standardly applies to cases where one has, or comes to have, a concept, a vision, an idea, an impression, a notion, a conception, a thought, a percept, etc., of a thing. There has thus been a shift in the meaning of the word. In the eighteenth century its core sense was intimately connected with the notion of reference. To have *Erkenntnis* of a thing was to have in one's mind a presentation, an idea, an image, a token referring to that thing.

This is in keeping with yet earlier usage. Leibniz had thought that the German word *Kenntnis* would be a good equivalent of the Latin *terminus simplex.*[10] The suggestion of Leibniz places the word *Kenntnis* in opposition to judgment: it is a *term* of judgment, not itself judgmental. Similarly, Wolff had used the expression as pertaining to concepts and terms rather than to judgments. "When we represent a thing to ourselves, we recognize it (*erkennen*). When our concepts are distinct, then our cognition (*Erkenntnis*) is distinct too."[11]

Translation of *Erkenntnis* as "knowledge" is appropriate much of the time, but not because Kant used the word in the contemporary sense, but because, quite generally, knowledge was then thought to be a felicitous kind of representation, a sort of successful reference. We might call it the Adamic Language Theory of knowledge: If one represented an object in one's mind by a kind of token that was really fitting, in the way in which the names that Adam gave to things were the real names of things, then one was thought to be as close to knowing the thing as was humanly possible. This makes understandable the close connection in eighteenth-century philosophy between good reference and knowledge: To know is to have a good picture, the right concept, the correct name, of a thing. Hence also the appropriateness of translating *Erkenntnis* as "knowledge" on many occasions. Nonetheless, reading it always as "knowledge" not only leads to absurdities, but effectively bars one's understanding of central concerns of the *Critique.*

Our text shows that Kant wanted to use the term *Erkenntnis* much in the way in which Leibniz had suggested: We note that the two subdivisions under the term are intuitions and concepts, i.e., singular and general terms. Other of Kant's writings reinforce this view of what *Erkenntnis* is. For example, in the transcript of his logic lectures which has come to us under the title *Vienna Logic,* Kant is quoted as saying that only the *connection* of cognitions constitutes a judgment. This means, of course, that a cognition is, as Leibniz had suggested, a *terminus simplex* which only in combination with other such terms will yield a judgment. Hence, properly understood, a cognition is a mental *term.* Again, in the *Logic* he repeats the division of cognitions into intuitions (singular) and concepts (general), thereby implying again that they are mental terms, not judgments. "Knowledge," by contrast, seems to require the presence of a judgment: "He knows that P" implies "He judges that P."

It might be thought that the change I am proposing would not greatly affect our understanding of the substance of the *Critique.* I will now try to show that it does, and that it is rather important to see this, particularly since *Erkenntnis* in present German usage is liable to the same sorts of misunderstanding as the English "knowledge."

There is, for example, a famous passage in the Transcendental Deduction in the First Edition, which Kemp Smith translates as follows: "It is only when we have thus produced synthetic unity in the manifold of intuition that we are in a position to say that we know the object."[12] This translation is faulty in several ways: Kemp Smith gives us the converse of the conditional stated by Kant, adds several words, and, of course, translates *erkennen* as "to know." A better reading of the sentence would be this: "We say that we recognize (discern, make out, make reference to) an object whenever we have produced synthetic unity in the manifold of intuition." Perhaps Kant intends a biconditional: An object is recognized if, and only if, a synthetic unity is produced. The point is that there would *be* no object without such a synthesis, not that the object would be unknown, or perhaps only partially or insufficiently known. Without the synthesis, the manifold of representations would simply fail to refer altogether: They would be like sensations, indeed, they would simply *be* sensations. Kant is concerned to explain how we come to have objects, make reference to objects, not how we come to know objects.

There are many other passages in which the translation of *Erkenntnis* as "cognition" or "reference" or the like would be more felicitous than rendering it as "knowledge." Still, one might argue that in view of the close connection between knowledge and reference in eighteenth-century thought no major exegetic problem will arise. Against this I now want to show that one of the grander themes of Kant's theoretical philosophy is obscured, and indeed made incomprehensible, by a failure to understand what *Erkenntnis* is.

It is well known that Kant thought the derivation of the table of categories from the table of judgments to be one of his major achievements. In the long footnote to the Preface of the *Metaphysical Principles of Science* he considers the "satisfactoriness of the table of categories as determinations of consciousness (which are) derived from the logical functions in judgments to be essential for the main purpose of the system."[13] By contrast, and somewhat surprisingly, he calls the Transcendental Deduction, usually considered the very core of the *Critique*, "in no way necessary, but merely meritorious."[14] Kant's early adherents tended to regard the Metaphysical Deduction as an integral and sound part of his system, while the balance of recent critical opinion considers the connection between judgments and categories questionable. Kemp Smith, for example, maintained that "Kant is unable to prove, and does not ultimately profess to prove, that it is the same operations, which are exercised in discursive and in creative thinking."[15] He denied that there is "identity or even analogy" between the functions exercised in judgments and the categories.[16] R. P. Wolff holds that the argument is "arbitrary in the extreme. The appearance from nowhere of the table of judgments and the rather flimsy argument of the table of categories are entirely unconvincing."[17]

It seems to me, however, that Kant's point is not so arbitrary. In his own brief comment on the *Critique* which I just cited he defines a judgment as an "act through which given representations first become cognitions of an object."[18] If we follow Kemp Smith in reading *Erkenntnis* as "knowledge," this reduces to the rather innocent claim, mentioned above, that all knowledge requires judgment, which can amount to no more than that knowledge is propositional, or that all knowledge is "knowledge that." What Kant wants to say, instead, is that the emergence of reference or intentionality requires judgments, and that without the operation of judging there would be no objects at all.

Kant was not alone in this view. Closely related views had been held by Condillac, Reid, Tetens, and probably others. There is also an obvious similarity to Frege's claim "that one must always have a complete sentence in view. Only within it have words properly a meaning. (*Bedeutung*)."[19] In *Tractatus* 3.3, Wittgenstein makes the related point that "only in the context of a sentence does a name have reference."

Kant did not think that the mere collecting together of sensational elements creates in itself the relation to an object. It is a necessary, but not a sufficient, condition for reference. What is needed, in addition, is the "recognition in a concept," or the bringing of the synthesis to concepts. But to recognize something in a concept is to make a judgment about it, to fit a predicate to it. It is only thus that the mind comes to refer to objects and that objects come into being for the mind.

The point of the Metaphysical Deduction is now not difficult to grasp. If there are several distinct and irreducible types of judgment, and if the very existence to the mind of objects depends upon the occurrence of judgments, then we may expect there to be equally many distinct and irreducible types of object. Hence a complete table of judgments will in effect give us a complete table of categories. It is the business of the Transcendental Deduction to show that there could be no reference, i.e., no object, without the activity of the understanding, not that there could be no *knowledge* without the understanding (this follows as a corollary). Later on, Kant thought that he could have dispensed entirely with the Transcendental Deduction if he had troubled himself a little more with giving a precise definition of the concept of a judgment, which would include that judgments are *constitutive* of objects and, presumably, that their forms therefore determine the forms of being.[20] Just to bring home my point, I conclude with a quotation from the Metaphysical Deduction in which I have systematically replaced Kemp Smith's translation of *Erkenntnis* and *erkennen* as "knowledge" and "to know" by "reference," "referring thought," and "to refer," as required. Kant says:

> By synthesis in its most general sense, I understand the act of putting different representations together, and to unite them into one referring thought. . . . Synthesis of a manifold . . . is what first gives rise to reference. . . . The synthesis is that which actually gathers the elements for referring thoughts and unites them to form a certain content. It is to synthesis, therefore, that we must first direct our attention, if we would determine the first origin of reference. [Actually *unserer Erkenntnis,* i.e., "the reference we make (to objects)."] Synthesis in general, as we shall hereafter see, is the mere result of the power of imagination, a blind but indispensable function of the soul, without which there would be no reference to anything, but of which we are scarcely ever conscious. To bring this synthesis to *concepts* is a function which belongs to the understanding, and it is this function of the understanding that first provides us with reference properly so called.[21]

This passage shows clearly that we cannot really hope to understand this central concern of the *Critique* if we do not attend to the proper rendition of *Erkenntnis* as "reference" or the like, or, in German, by such a word as, perhaps, *Gegenstandsbezug*.

NOTES

1 *Logic,* A41/42.

2 Vol. 24.2, p. 565.

3 *Versuch einer neuen Theorie des menschlichen Vorstellungsvermögens* (Prag and Jena, 1789), p. 224.

4 Johann Christian Gottsched, *Erste Gründe der gesammten Weltweisheit,* 6th ed. (Leipzig, 1750), pp. 524ff.

5 Cf. *Monadology,* no. 60, *Principles of Nature and Grace,* no. 2.

6 Cf. my "Transcendental Object and Thing in Itself," *Akten des 4. Internationalen Kant Kongresses* (Mainz, 1974), 2, p. 1.

7 Refl. 695.

8 C.P.R. A189/B234.

9 Johann Christian Adelung, *Grammatisch-Kritisches Wörterbuch der Hochdeutschen Mundart* (Leipzig, 1793), p. 1906.

10 G. W. Leibniz, *Deutsche Schriften,* ed. G. E. Guhrauer (Berlin, 1838), p. 379.

11 *Vernünftige Gedanken von Gott, der Welt und der Seele des Menschen* ("German Metaphysics"), 5th ed. (Frankfurt and Leipzig, 1731), p. 466.

12 A105/B135.

13 AXVI.

14 Ibid.

15 *Commentary,* p. 177.

16 *Commentary,* p. 179.

17 *Kant's Theory of Mental Activity* (Boston, 1963), p. 77.

18 *Metaphysical Principles of Science,* pp. xix, xx.

19 *Grundlagen,* p. 71.

20 *Metaphysical Principles of Science,* xix, xx.

21 A77/B103 f.

MOLTKE S. GRAM

The Sense of a Kantian Intuition

A Kantian *Anschauung* is a designation of a philological problem that can be solved only by philosophical argument. Lexicographical appeals to the linguistic equivalence of *Anschauung* with its English counterpart "intuition" merely exchange one semantical label for another. They do not solve the problem. We cannot measure the adequacy of this translation because Kant's use of the word, while it is compatible with the standard, received sense in German, is still too narrow to be captured accurately by that usage. There remains a variety of alternatives each of which yields a different view of the notion of intuition in Kant's theory of knowledge and ontology. Nor does an appeal to the philosophical use of the term in Kant's time get us any further. His contemporaries found Kant's use of the term as objectionable as many of us find it baffling. And, finally, the Anglo-Saxon translational tradition merely aggravates an already critical problem by insinuating alien philosophical doctrines into Kant's text only to extract an interpretation of the notion which lacks an independent confirmation outside the theory dictating the translation.

The fact is that we lack a more appropriate word to translate *Anschauung* into English than the one now at our disposal. For we lack at present the conditions which any such substitution must satisfy in order to count as an adequate translation. Consider first the philosophical muddle which many of Kant's Anglo-Saxon translators have bequeathed us.

Moltke S. Gram is professor of philosophy, University of Iowa, Iowa City.

1   *The Anglo-Saxon Connection*

The mischief begins with J. Hutchison Stirling, who translates *Anschauung* as "perception" in his *Textbook to Kant*.[1] He translates *Vorstellung* as "intimation."[2] The philological damage (*horribile dictu*) is lamentable enough. But it is compounded by a philosophical error. Stirling inserts an admonition into his translation. He tells us that we will not understand Kant's language if we give to such words "no reference but the usual intellectual one of thought proper as opposed to sense."[3] He explains by distinguishing between what he calls crude and complete perception, saying that crude perception "is these [space and time] inspissated, by special sensations, into *Erscheinungen,* which are objects, but as yet without the foci of the categories. Complete or finished perception, lastly, is by addition of action from the categories, the ordinary perception of experience proper."[4] He assures us that "[w]hatever has that character in it — beyond mere sensation — of sensible discernibleness, perceptivity, objectivity, is an *Anschauung.*" He concludes: "[A]n *Anschauung,* a perception, is only crude and elementary when . . . the sensible details of it alone stand before consciousness."[5] Thus Stirling.

Stirling is not alone in this unfortunate adventure. Edward Caird joins him when he says this: *"Anschauung* I have generally translated by 'Perception,' rarely by 'intuition.'"[6] But what about *Wahrnehmung?* "Sense-perception," Caird continues, is how he renders the German "wherever . . . it seemed necessary to call attention to its contrast with *Anschuung.*"[7] And this misadventure does not stop here. The philological-cum-philosophical miscarriage survives to the present. Stephen Körner professes to use the term "almost synonymously with that of 'perception' (*Wahrnehmung*)."[8] And T. D. Weldon follows him in this.[9]

This translational crotchet has not perverted the entire Anglo-Saxon interpretation of *Anschauung.* Neither the Max Müller nor the Kemp Smith translation of the first *Kritik* conflates Kantian intuitions with perceptions. But they do not offer to explain what an intuition is. They are silent about why they have departed from the entrenched practice of Anglo-Saxon translation. They have succeeded in avoiding the pitfalls of their predecessors and successors. They have not, however, justified their own gloss.[10]

But what, exactly, is wrong with the Stirling translation? Why should we not be content to translate *Anschauung* as "perception," and, heeding the Stirling distinction between crude and finished perception, concede that the term can be translated in that way? Just this: The translation obliterates the distinction between perception (*Wahrnehmung*) and intuition (*Anschauung*). Suppose that we cling to the Stirling gloss. Suppose we say that a Kantian intuition just *is* a perception. This commitment, as we will soon see, is three times fatal.

First. Such a commitment prevents us from explaining how space and time can be intuitions. Empirical intuitions are sensations. To say this for Kant is to say that they are the result of our sensory apparatus being affected by objects acting on it. But there are also pure intuitions. They are not sensations but rather the conditions under which our ability to have sensations is possible. They are not the result of our being affected by something else. But they are also intuitions. And this clashes with Kant's definition of perception. For he tells us that perception is a synthesis of sensations, that it is an intuition accompanied by sensation, and that it is just sensation accompanied by consciousness.[11] The notion of perception assumes the notion of intuition; hence, it cannot be identical with such a notion.

Second. The claim that intuition and perception are one and the same thing conflicts dramatically with Kant's claim that sensation is the matter of intuition.[12] To say that sensation is the matter of intuition assumes an independent specification of the notion of intuition in order to understand the notion of sensation. This has serious consequences for the putative equivalence of intuition with perception. Kant says flatly that perception is empirical consciousness that contains sensation.[13] But sensation is for Kant the effect of an object on our sensory apparatus.[14] This, again, is just to say that intuition is logically prior to perception.

Third. The description which Kant gives us of an intuition is logically independent of the description he gives of what he calls a perception. Recall the repeatedly basic account that Kant gives of perception. He says that it is empirical consciousness which contains sensation.[15] But the very notion of empirical consciousness assumes the existence of a Kantian intuition. Kant's own account of perception dramatizes this fact. Empirical consciousness contains sensation. But sensation is the matter of empirical intuition.[16] Once again the matter of sensation assumes intuition. It cannot without circularity give us an account of what an intuition is.

The objection to the Stirling gloss can be generalized. *If you take "intuition" to mean "perception," you make it impossible to distinguish between an act by which we synthesize a manifold and the act by which we apprehend each member of the manifold.* The former cannot take place without the latter. But once you start calling an intuition a perception, you succeed only in obliterating the distinction between an intuition and a concept. For you are not going to be able to distinguish between an intuition and a concept when you have already appropriated a word which designates something involved in both. And so, accept Stirling's substitution of "perception" for "intuition," and you move in a circle if you want to understand what a Kantian intuition is. The circle is this. You first say that what the rest of us call an intuition is really a perception. Then you say that a perception is an intuition together with something called conceptual awareness. And then, confronted with the inevitable question of what the intuition contained in the perception is, you are right back where you started.

Stirling's distinction between crude and finished perception is a textbook case of this kind of reasoning. That distinction is merely a verbal fig leaf for what in fact takes place in his assimilation of intuition to perception and perception to intuition. To say, as Stirling does, that intuition is just crude perception is to say no more than that it is an intuition. To say, as Stirling also does, that a perception is a finished perception is only to say that it is what it is — a perception. This merely restores the original distinction to its integrity while making Kant's text and his theory suffer from the legerdemain which animates the philosophical blunder.

2   *Kant's Conditions*

So perception (*Wahrnehmung*) is not the same thing as intuition (*Anschauung*). This much insight is not enough, however, to get us out of the woods. The Kantian text itself is anything but clear about what an intuition is. Begin with the *Inaugural Dissertation*. Kant says:

> Intellectualiam non datur (homini) intuitus sed nonnisi *cognitio symbolica,* et intellectio tantum licet per conceptus universales in abstracto, non per singularem in concreto. Omnis enim intuitus noster adstringitur cuidam formae, sub qua sola aliquid immediate, s. ut *singulare,* a mente *cerni* et non tantum discursive per conceptus generales concipi potest.[17]

> [There is not given (to man) an *intuition* of things intellectual, but only a *symbolic cognition,* and intellection is only allowable for us through universal concepts in the abstract and not through a singular concept in the concrete. For all our intuition is bound to a certain principle of form under which form alone can be *discerned* by the mind immediately or as *singular,* and not merely conceived discursively through general concepts.]

Kant continues:

> Intuitus autem purus (humanus) non est conceptus universalis s. logicus, *sub quo,* sed singularis, *in quo* sensibilis quaelibet cogitantur, ideoque continet spatii et tempris . . . . [18]

> [But pure (human) intuition is not a universal or logical concept *under which,* but is a singular concept *in which,* sensibles no matter what are thought, and so it contains the concepts of space and time.]

What we are told here is this. An intuition is a kind of concept. It is an individual concept as distinct from a concept of a common property. And, finally, what distinguishes an individual from a general concept is that things are contained in the former but fall under the latter.

All of this is a hermeneutical nightmare that has visited Anglo-Saxon and German philosophy alike ever since it was written. Consider first the notion of an individual concept. Kant rejects the very notion elsewhere as a redundancy.[19] But this is misleading. If Kant is right, it is not a redundancy at all but rather a blatant contradiction. Whatever else it may be, a Kantian concept is something that is predicable of many.[20] To argue that it is logically possible for some concepts to be predicable of one and only one subject does not remove the difficulty. A concept constitutionally predicable of one and only one subject would obliterate the distinction between a concept and an intuition. And this would illegitimately transform a Kantian intuition into a concept.

Even worse is to come. The distinction between falling within and falling under something aggravates an already precarious attempt to disclose the nature of an intuition. The concept, ". . . is green," is contained under the concept, ". . . is a color." And some concepts fall within other concepts. The concept of ". . . is rational" falls within the concept of ". . . is a man." True, one intuition cannot be contained under another intuition. But this still does not advance our understanding of a Kantian intuition. The same relation can obtain between one *concept* and another. We must, accordingly, be able to say how the relation of falling under distinguishes intuitions from concepts and, further, what there is about an intuition that prevents it from falling under another intuition although it must also be capable of being contained under a concept.

The first *Kritik* account goes further. There Kant says:

> Auf welche Art und durch welche Mittel sich auch immer eine Erkenntnis auf Gegenstände beziehen mag, es ist doch diejenige, wodurch sie sich auf

dieselbe unmittelbar bezieht, und worauf alles Denken als Mittel abzweckt, die *Anschauung*. . . . Vermittelst der Sinnlichkeit also werden uns Gegenstände *gegeben,* und sie allein liefert uns *Anschauungen.* [21]

[In whatever manner and by whatever means a mode of knowledge may relate to objects, *intuition* is that through which it is in immediate relation to them, and to which all thought as means is directed. . . . Objects are *given* to us by means of sensibility, and they alone give us intuitions.]

Kant expands:

Eine *Perception,* die sich lediglich auf das Subjekt, als die Midifikation seines Zustandes bezieht, ist *Empfindung* (sensatio), eine objektive Perception ist *Erkenntnis* (cognitio). Diese ist entweder *Anschauung* oder *Begriff* (intuitivus vel conceptus). Jene bezieht sich unmittelbar auf den Gegenstand und ist einzeln; dieser mittelbar, vermittelst eines Merkmals, was mehreren Dingen gemein sein kann. [22]

[A *perception* which relates solely to the subject as the modification of its state is *sensation* (*sensatio*), an objective perception is *knowledge* (*cognitio*). This is either *intuition* or *concept* (*intuitus vel conceptus*). The former relates immediately to the object and is single, the latter refers to it mediately by means of a feature which several things have in common.]

The philological difficulties begin here. And they point to the philosophical difficulties permeating Kant's terminology.

Kant begins by distinguishing between an intuition and a concept in terms of two kinds of *concept.* A Kantian intuition is, accordingly, what Kant calls a singular concept. The case for the existence of intuitions would seem to rest entirely on whether there really are individual concepts. But then he changes his principle of division and states the distinction between concepts and intutions in terms, not of concepts, but of *representations.* The substitution of "representation" for "concept" resolves the problem of internal inconsistency. It also mars the concept-intuition distinction in another and equally objectionable way. All representations just insofar as they are representations are individual episodes in somebody's mental history. But this fact leaves us with the problem of specifying the criterion for distinguishing singular from general representations. Without such a criterion Kant will have forfeited the very distinction he wants to make. Supposing an intuition to be a distinctive kind of mental *act,* then, blurs the distinction between an intuition and a concept as badly as its predecessor. We can, for one thing, make the same distinction between two different states of enlightenment about a concept that we can make with respect to intuitions. We can be acquainted with the elements of an intuition just as we can be aware of the elements of a concept in various degrees. For another, the account enables us only to make true statements about our epistemic relation to intuitions. It does not tell us what is to be an intuition.

The counterevidence is initially persuasive. It comes directly from Kant's mouth. He tells us that intuitions and concepts are parts of the same thing.[23] And he repeatedly lays it down that there are individual concepts.[24] Neither works. Yes, Kant does say that intuitions and concepts are parts of the same thing—namely, cognition (*Erkenntnis*). Both of them are representations (*Vorstellungen*). But this does not imply that representations of individuals are individual concepts.

Kant's explicit claim that intuitions are individual concepts is more intractable to reconstruction than its predecessor. But does his claim that there are concepts which have one and only one object falling under them transform intuitions into a kind of concept? Emphatically not. Both philosophical and philological reasons argue against it. A Kantian concept is something that is definitionally common to many. Thus a concept that is instantiated by one and only one entity is a successful candidate for self-contradiction.[25]

But this is not all. Kant's *Logik* tells us that, not concepts themselves, but only their *use* can be divided into general and individual.[26] A concept may, then, be *used* to single out one and only one entity. This does not, however, imply the contradiction that there are concepts which are not predicable of many any more than it transforms intuitions into a kind of concept. It implies only that we deploy concepts in situations in which we identify intuitions. And this is compatible with the basic definition of a concept as being common to many because it transfers singularity of identification to the context in which the concept is applied.

3   Anschauungen: *Another Attempt*

All of this still leaves us without an understanding of what a Kantian intuition is. Suppose temporarily that the concept-intuition distinction is really the difference between what has been called knowledge by acquaintance and knowledge by description.[27] Let us say that we know something by acquaintance whenever we are directly aware of it.[28] And, further, say that we know something by description whenever we know that something has certain properties, even though whatever has those properties is not presented to us in experience.[29]

The alternative is initially attractive. One of the conditions of knowing something by description is that we know truths about it. This involves knowing that it falls under certain predicates or concepts. The acquaintance-description distinction might, therefore, be the philosophical basis for explicating Kant's concept-intuition distinction.

But is it? I think not. It nonetheless fails, albeit instructively. For one thing, the distinction between acquaintance and description does not separate our awareness of the objects of intuition and concepts. We can be acquainted with concepts just as we can be acquainted with the particulars that fall under them."[30] For there can be concepts which we grasp on one occasion by means of truths about them, only to be directly aware of them on another occasion. For another, we can know anything in either the mode of acquaintance or description. We can know objects of intuition by acquaintance or by description. And, as we have just seen, we can know one and the same particular in each mode for just the same reason. The acquaintance-description distinction may be genuine. But it is useless in interpreting the intuition-concept distinction. That distinction applies across the board just because we can have mediate awareness of objects of intuition as much as we can be immediately aware of concepts.

It would be futile to argue that we intuit the subject of a judgment and conceive of the properties which we believe it to have. This reconstruction assimilates intuition to perception. When you make an intuition into a kind of perception, you tacitly and illegitimately rely on the concept-intuition distinction by using it in your explication. True, a Kantian intuition is a case of perceptual consciousness. Kant says so himself.[31] But if you appeal to the generic notion of perceptual consciousness in your attempt to distinguish intuitions from concepts, you merely assume the very discussion which you are supposed to be explicating. You assume it just because there is a relation between an intuition and a concept within the context of this kind of cognition. For the relation here holds between a perceptual particular and its properties.

The philological headache does not stop here. Kant also says that an intuition is a perceptual object in which we can be aware without perceiving it under any description. This emerges in the Jäsche version of Kant's *Logik:*

In every cognition there is to be distinguished *matter,* i.e. the object, and *form,* i.e. the manner *how* we cognize the object. For example, when a savage sees a house in the distance, the use of which he does not know, he has the same object before him as another who knows it as a dwelling furnished for man.

But as to form, this cognition of one and the same object is different in both. In the one it is *mere intuition,* in the other *intuition* and *concept* at the same time.[32]

[In jeder Erkenntnis muss unterschieden werden Materie, d.i. der Gegenstand, und Form, d.i. die Art, wei wir den Gegenstand erkennen. Sieht z. B. ein Wilder ein Haus aus der Ferne, dessen Begrauch er nicht kennt: so hat er zwar eben dasselbe Object wie ein Anderer, der es bestimmt als eine für Menschen eingerichtete Wohnung kennt, in der Vorstellung vor sich. Aber der Form nach ist dieses Erkenntnis eines und desselben Objects in beiden verschieden. Bei dem Einen ist es *blosse Anschauung,* bei dem Andern Anschauung und *Begriff* zugleich.]

Whenever we perceive something without subsuming it under a concept, we intuit it. Otherwise we conceive it. There is no intimation here of the distinction between singular or general representations. We are told only that an intuition is a perception and, further, that it is a kind of perception in which objects are not subsumed under concepts.

This only replaces one difficulty with another. Kant's example is defective. And the implicit explanation of the concept-intuition distinction supporting it breaks down on a contradiction. Take the example first. The perceptual states of the savage and somebody else are merely different states of enlightenment about the same object. The savage still perceives the house under some description or other, even though he is ignorant of its function. The difference then is not between perceiving something under a description and perceiving that thing without subsuming it under any description at all. The example illustrates cases of perceiving one thing under two descriptions. This makes both cases of perceptual consciousness judgmental. Once again the concept-intuition distinction deliquesces.

So much for Kant's example. One stubborn fact remains: Both cases of awareness are acts of *perceiving.* And this makes both of them acts of judgment. This, in turn, requires that both be instances of subsuming something under a concept. The distinction between an intuition and a concept is reproduced in each case. This, in turn, merely perpetuates the problem of making the distinction without solving it.

4 *New Bearings*

Kant has told us that an intuition is a kind of concept, that it stands in a unique relation to entities called concepts, and finally even that it is a kind of judgment. None of these glosses is either philologically

accurate or philosophically defensible. To say that an intuition is
really an individual concept only postpones the inevitable difficulty.
Individual concepts may be peculiar because one and only one object
falls under them. *But it is with respect to this one-and-only-one thing which
falls under a concept that we want to know what distinguishes it from a concept.* Kant's appeal to the peculiarity of individual concepts is silent
about this. All of this may be true of intuitions. But Kantian concepts can satisfy the same condition, and even if we waive this difficulty we must still account for what makes the one-and-only-one
object that falls under an individual concept different from the concept under which it falls. What is wanted is an explanation of what
makes the object falling under the concept different from the concept
under which it is subsumed and not what makes it the one-and-only-
one object falling under that concept. The distinction between two
kinds of perceptual awareness has proved to be equally futile. If we
say that the concept-intuition distinction is really the difference between what has been called knowledge by acquaintance and knowledge by description, we succeed only in specifying two ways in which
one and the same entity can be cognitively available. We do not
show that there are two kinds of *entity* which are cognitively available,
each in its own way.

All of these distinctions may be legitimate. All of them may be
truly applicable to the concept-intuition distinction. But one recalcitrant fact remains: None of them can give us a *definition* of a Kantian
intuition without either moving in a circle or making it into something that it is not. There are still three sources which potentially
provide the basis for a reconstruction of that notion: namely, the
linguistic tradition which Kant inherits; the use made of the notion
by his immediate philosophical predecessors and contemporaries;
and, finally, what his own contemporaneous commentators attribute
to him. Take them in turn.

First, the tradition of German usage. The northern mystical tradition introduced the word into the language in the late Middle Ages
as *anschouungo, Anschouung,* or *anscouuen.* It specified a kind of awareness that does not involve concepts or, what comes to the same, a
beatific vision as over against discursive cognition.[33] Later the word
came to be used for sensation (*Empfindung*) as over against what was
called symbolic (*figürlich*) knowledge, which depends on the use of
conventional or natural signs.[34] And, finally, Johann Christoph
Adelung tells us in his *Grammatischkritisches Wörterbuch der hochdeutschen
Mundart* (Vienna: B. Ph. Bauer, 1811) under the entry for *Anschauen:*

"In weiterer Bedeutung wird dieses Wort auch überhaupt für emp-
finden gebraucht, ohne dasselbe auf die Empfindung des Sehens allein
einzuschränken." [This word is used in an extended sense for sensation in general without being restricted to visual sensation.] Adelung
continues: "[I]n der Philosophie verstehet man durch die anschauende
Erkenntnis, eine jede Erkenntnis, die wir durch die Empfindung er-
langen, oder da wir uns die Sache selbst oder doch ihr Bild vorstellen,
die sinnliche, bildliche Erkenntnis, im Gegensatz zum symbolischen,
da man eine Sache unter Worten oder anderen Zeichen denkt."[35] [In
philosophy intuitive knowledge is understood as that knowledge that
we gain by sensation or, since we represent to ourselves the thing
itself or even its image, sensuous, pictorial as opposed to symbolic
knowledge, since something is thought by means of words or other
signs.] And Grimm complains (entry, *Anschauen*) that "Dies wort
haven die philosophen dem Sprachgebrauch ohne noth erschwert.
anschauen erstreckt sich zuerst auf sinnliche, dann auf übersinnliche,
geistige gegenstände. . . ."[36] [Philosophers have used this word to
make linguistic usage unnecessarily difficult. "Intuition" encompasses
primarily sensuous and then supersensuous, intellectual objects.]

This exercise in historical semantics nets us next to nothing. Jaakko
Hintikka tells us that the ordinary usage of the term in German is
historically unstable and concludes that it is not a reliable guide to
Kant's use of the word.[37]　True, but for the wrong reasons. The
term does have a unified acceptation in the history of the German
language.　It designates nondiscursive as distinct from discursive
awarenesses. This usage was preserved when it came to mark the
contrast between symbolic or figurative knowledge and immediate
awareness even when, as the brothers Grimm remind us, philosophers
extended that distinction to all objects of sensation and even to the
awareness of nonsensuous objects. The context in which the term is
used does change; but the basic distinction between nondiscursive
and discursive apprehension is the Ariadne's thread connecting those
contexts.

Discontinuity is not, however, the relevant problem with an appeal
to historical semantics. That appeal is defective. The results are too
vague to accommodate the refinements of sense which Kant attaches
to the term. Kant's usage is compatible with the linguistic tradition.
But we do not learn whether an intuition is an individual concept,
whether it relates to a concept by being contained under rather than
within it, or whether it can be specified independently of any reference
to sensation at all.

The tradition of ordinary German usage lacks the semantical resources to solve our problem.   The philosophical tradition which presided over Kant's development tells another story.   Alexander Gottfried Baumgarten's *Metaphysica,* a text which Kant frequently used in his lectures, explicates the concept-intuition distinction this way:

> Si signum & signatum percipiendo coniungitur, & maior est signi, quam signati perceptio, *cognitio* talis *symbolica* dicitur, si maior signati repraesentatio, quam signi, *cognitio* erit *intuitiva* (intuitus). [38]

> [If sign and signatum are perceptually conjoined and the perception of the sign is prior to that of the signatum, it is called *symbolic cognition.* If the representation of the signatum is prior to that of the sign, it will be *intuitive cognition.*]

What is completely determined is a singular or individual: "complexus omnium determinationum in ente compossibilium est *omnimoda* eius *determinatio.*" [The complex of all that is compossibily determinate in a thing is its *complete determination.*]   The difference between an individual and a universal or common property, then, is the number of determinations or predicates that applies to each.

Christian August Crusius puts it differently: We represent to ourselves what he calls an "idea singularis stricte sic dicta" [a singular idea strictly so called] whenever we form a concept which can be predicated of one and only one individual. [40]   Friedrich Meier tangles an already anarchic tradition when he traces our representations of singulars to *anschauende Urteile* [intuitive judgments].   These in turn are reduced to claims about immediate experience.   They are one and all *einzelne Urteile* [individual judgments]. [41]   Christian Wolff perturbs the tradition even more by distinguishing what he calls *figürliche Erkäntnis* [figurative cognition] from *anschauende Erkäntnis* [intuitive knowledge]. [42]   In the former, he explains, we represent something to ourselves by means of words or other signs; in the latter, by the things themselves.

This is what Kant inherited from his immediate predecessors. He was acquainted with all of the works I have canvassed.   He also regularly used several of them as textbooks for his lectures.   All of them use the same language as Kant in order to distinguish between symbolic and intuitive cognition.   For Kant's predecessors agreed that singulars are objects of intuitive cognition.   But they all leave something out.   None of them distinguishes a *particular* from an *individual.* Without this distinction we cannot understand the crucial change which took place in philosophical semantics when Kant broke through to his distinction between intuitions and concepts. Let me explain.

Both an individual and a particular can be the referent of a definite description. Any concept qualifies as an individual. Thus Frege's legendary example, "The concept 'horse' is a concept easily attained." Any concept can be the object of either symbolic or intuitive cognition. So far from preserving the distinction between our acquaintance with a singular and our acquaintance with a common predicate or concept, Kant's immediate predecessors merely obliterate the very distinction they were trying to secure. A Kantian concept can function as an object of immediate or mediate awareness. Think otherwise and you will confuse the *function* of something in a judgment with the kind of *entity* it is. Something may function as a predicate in one judgment and still serve as the subject of another judgment. This says nothing about whether it is a concept or an intuition. All it *does* say is that the mediate-immediate distinction applies to concepts and intuitions alike.

This leaves us with our third source of appeal. How did Kant's early expositors interpret the notion of an intuition? The accounts available to us constitute a hermeneutical jungle. Sometimes we are told that an intuition is whatever is grasped immediately through affection.[43] Then we are asked to believe that an intuition is a concept which designates one and only one object.[44] Sometimes the sources say that an intuition is just a sensation.[45] The already entangled critical tradition is worsened when we are told that an intuition is a judgment of experience whereas a concept is a judgment of perception.[46] Finally, an intuition is alleged to be a direct representation of an individual object as it is in itself through properties.[47]

Which alternative squares with the way in which Kant actually uses the notion of intuition? First, the immediacy account. It may be *true* to say that an intuition is whatever is grasped immediately. This cannot, however, define an intuition. Whenever we grasp something immediately, we are acquainted with it without having had to be aware of something else and then inferring to the existence of what we claim to grasp. One part of the tradition reports that we grasp something intuitively whenever we dispense with the use of figurative or symbolic knowing. Here the tradition begins to falter. It fails to distinguish between grasping a concept and grasping something by means of a concept. The distinction is as palmary as its consequences are disastrous. One stubborn fact remains: The mediate-immediate distinction can apply to our awareness of concepts just as it applies to our awareness of the nonconceptual denizens of the world. I am not denying that Kant says an intuition is whatever is grasped immediately. I claim only that this strand of the tradition confuses a true *statement* about an intuition with a *definition* of what an intuition is. We might, for all Kant says, grasp a concept immediately. But this does not imply that we must always grasp it by means of a further concept. The same holds for our epistemic relation to Kantian intuitions.

But what about the view that what Kant calls an intuition is an individual concept? This is a textually formidable candidate. We have already seen that Kant's immediate predecessors interpreted *Anschauung* in this way. We have also seen that Kant himself sometimes equates intuitions with individual concepts. And, finally, some of the *Kantianer* contemporaneous with Kant interpret the term in that way. The argument for this rendering runs as follows. Intuitions are elements of our knowledge. The knowledge of which they are elements is propositional. The fundamental description of *Anschauung* includes the relation it has to its object. That relation is one of reference. Therefore, intuitions are concepts.[48]

That, then, is a schematic statement of the argument for assimilating intuitions to individual concepts. But the position is self-destructive. The very notion of an individual concept would seem to be a contradiction in terms just because a concept for Kant, whatever else it may be, is at least something that is common to several objects. And so, to say that there are representations that are individual concepts would just be to say that there are conceptual representations which refer to one and only one object. But this clashes with the definition of a concept as something which can be multiply instantiated.[49]

The difficulty can be removed. We might reformulate the notion of an individual concept.[50] Let us speak of expressions and their intensions. Some expressions have intensions that designate properties and relations. Others are associated with designators which are intensions of individual expressions. The use of the notion of a designator avoids the verbal contradiction which would otherwise make it impossible to give this alternative the hearing for which there is massive evidence.

Very well, then. We agree to understand by "individual concept" any expression the intension of which designates one and only one entity. But the semantical cosmetics do not conceal the profound difficulties that remain. We are faced with the problem of explicating the notion of an individual intension. Suppose we say that that linguistic expression designating individuals uniquely have intensions.

This would require us to say that names entail some attributes which their bearers necessarily have. The sense of a name would then be explicated partially in terms of whatever properties that the individual it designates necessarily has. These allegedly make the designator an intuition rather than a concept. But they also beg the question. The claim that in intuition is what it is in virtue of the fact that it has a property or properties which it and no other object necessarily has merely introduces the notion of a predicate and with it the notion of a concept all over again. Predicates are concepts. Even if we chose to ignore this defect, another would replace it. The same argument could be used to show that designators of concepts denote one and only one concept just in virtue of the fact that each of them necessarily implies at least one unique predicate. This attempt at a solution only perpetuates the problem it is supposed to solve.

So let us abandon the view that a name is a Kantian intuition because of the intension it has. Suppose we say that a name singles out a particular just in virtue of its being a label that attaches to that and no other particular. The meaning of the name consists in the fact that it designates one and only one particular. Properties or concepts would not be involved, whether as predicates necessarily following from the intension of the name or as properties belonging to the referent of the name. The alternative is only vacuously true. Some words admittedly can be *used* to designate uniquely; but this still does not tell us what a Kantian intuition is. For one thing, words for concepts can perform this function just as words for particulars do. The word, say, which designates something that is brown is as unique a designator as the word which designates the concept of brownness. For another, the account is question begging. It assumes that proper names can be distinguished from predicate terms because the former, unlike the latter, designate singulars rather than common properties. And this assumes an independent argument for the distinction between singulars and common properties. It cannot be used to explicate that distinction.

But what if individual concepts are not names at all? What if they are definite descriptions? Suppose that an individual concept has the linguistic garb of "The . . . " where what fills the place marker is a designator of some concept. The grammatical subject of the description is transformed into a logical predicate, and what functions referentially are the quantifiers, which, as we all know, designate particulars. This alternative would admittedly have the advantage of explaining how an individual concept is not self-contradictory, because the conceptual element in sentences whose subject terms are definite descriptions would be remanded to the predicate place in the propositions in which they occur. They no longer denote. What *does* denote is the logical subject term of the proposition. And this is logically separated from the predicate of the proposition in which it occurs.

There is a fatal difficulty here. This alternative still requires that we grasp whatever we intuit by means of concepts. And this would destroy the very distinction that Kant wants to make. Whatever else it may be, intuiting is not grasping by means of concepts. The appeal to definite descriptions leaves us, then, without a viable explanation of Kant's distinction.

The philosophical case against assimilating intuitions to individual concepts is conclusive. But it does not do away with the historical-cum-philological evidence. The fact remains: Kant occasionally talks about intuitions as though they were a kind of concept. The evidence for this is distressingly abundant. In the initial draft of the *Preisschrift über die Fortschritte der Metaphysik,* Kant says that conceptual knowledge is discursive; intuitive knowledge, intuitive. But he goes on to say that "in der That wird zu einer Erkenntnis beides mit einander verbunden erfordert."[51] [In fact both are required to be connected with each other in one judgment.] And this is not isolated. In the first *Kritik* he describes a judgment (*Erkenntnis*) and continues saying that a judgment "ist entweder *Anschauung* oder *Begriff* (intuitus vel conceptus)."[52] [. . . is either an *intuition* or a *concept* (intuitivus vel conceptus).] Nor was this a transitory tendency in Kant's philosophical career. He exhibits it as early as the *Inaugural Dissertation.*[53]

All of this initially flies in the face of any attempt to argue that an intuition is something other than a kind of concept.[54] But the evidence is worthless. The Kant of the *Preisschrift* admittedly says that intuition is *required* for a complete cognition. He does not say that being a concept is a necessary or even a sufficient condition for its being a constituent in a judgment. Nor does the Kant of the *Inaugural Dissertation* think otherwise. There we are told only that intuitions, unlike concepts, are singular *representations* (*repraesentationes,* not *conceptus!*). All of this, so far from supporting the claim that intuitions are individual concepts, is at most completely neutral about that issue.

So much for the individual concept theory of Kantian intuitions. Consider what I shall call the sensation theory. Kant distinguishes sensations (*Empfindungen*), which he calls subjective perceptions, from intuitions, which he calls objective perceptions.[55] And he extends the term *Anschauung* to cover both empirical and what he calls formal intuition.[56] Suppose temporarily that an empirical intuition *is* a sensation for the initially plausible reason that a Kantian sensation is the result of an object affecting our sensory apparatus.[57] But there is no relation of affection between things and our sensory apparatus when it comes to the pure forms of intuition. This is the fact on which the sensation theory of intuitions irrevocably breaks down. Kant cannot and does not hold that the forms of intuition are themselves what take place after we are affected by objects. The affection relation cannot, therefore, hold between objects and pure intuitions. It may be true, therefore, that sensations are intuitions. It is not true that they qualify as such just because they are sensations.

The critical tradition bequeaths us a terminal alternative. Suppose we seek to distinguish between an intuition and a concept by appealing to Kant's distinction between judgments of experience (*Erfahrungsurteile*) and judgments of perception (*Wahrnehmungsurteile*).[58] An intuition is thus a kind of knowledge because it at least is judgmental and is distinguished from conceptual awareness only in that the judgment involved is about events in our own mental history rather than events which take place independently of whatever goes on in that history. Kant allegedly gives us this clue. He says that there are judgments which report only what occurs in immediate sensory awareness. These, he says, are only subjectively valid. They are only so many reports about a perceptual life within us that may or may not agree with the events going on outside our several mental histories. But then there are judgments which involve a subsumption of the perceptions each of us has in his various mental histories under the categories. The former require only intuitions. But the latter require the deployment of concepts. Kant illustrates: If the sun shines on a stone, that stone grows warm. This is an expression of a judgment of perception because it is not necessarily and universally true. A judgment of this kind tells us only something about a connection of intuitions or, rather, how our perceptions are habitually connected.[59] But if a judgment gives us information about a necessary connection between two perceptions, it involves the relation between at least two empirical concepts and the category of causation.

The tradition fails us once again. The distinction between two kinds of judgment assumes that we already know what a Kantian intuition is in order to state the very distinction which is supposed to elucidate the concept-intuition distinction. Granted, judgments of experience may not relate the perceptions it combines to categories.

But this is not to say that such judgments fail to relate intuitions to any concepts at all. *The issue about the sense of a Kantian intuition arises with respect to each member of the series of perceptions whether those members be necessarily or only contingently related to one another.* There is nothing in the distinction between what Kant calls a subjective and an objective judgment to show that there is a distinction between an intuition and a concept. The distinction between two kinds of judgment pertains merely to the way in which we combine the intuitions we have. The intuition-concept distinction can be made with respect to any kind of combination of perceptions, subjective or objective. This approach to an understanding of a Kantian intuition fails, then, because it is based on two different relations which intuitions can stand to concepts. It does not explicate the notion of a Kantian intuition. It assumes an understanding of that notion as a necessary condition of its own intelligibility.

5   *Intuitions in Themselves*

We have seen that the notions of perception and intuition are not logically equivalent either in German or in English. We have also seen how attempts to make them logically equivalent saddle Kant with a question-begging account of intuition. The notion of perception cannot tell us what an intuition is because perceptions assume the existence of intuitions. And the notion of sensation has fared no better, for it too assumes the notion of intuition. Neither the linguistic nor the philosophical tradition has given us the information needed for a solution to this problem. Even though linguistic usage is consistent with Kant's use of the *Anschauung,* it is irremediably vague about the way in which Kant's use of the term fits into that pattern. The philosophical tradition fares no better. For it does not properly distinguish between a particular and an individual, and even the very distinctions which Kant himself employs to separate concepts from intuitions are deficient just because they apply as much to the relation of one intuition to another as they apply to the relation of one concept and another. This disqualifies them from being the basis of the distinction between a concept and an intuition. They may all truly describe that distinction. But none of them tells us what the nature of that distinction is.

The difficulties which I have been recording force us to examine the way in which Kant tries to establish that there are such entities rather than what he tells us that he is doing. Kant gives us two arguments for the existence of intuitions. They are the Argument from

Volumes and the Argument from Incongruous Counterparts.[60] The former runs like this:

1   We can represent to ourselves (*uns vorstellen*) only one space and time.[61] ʼ
2   Diverse spatial and temporal parts are, therefore, limitations (*Einschränkungen*) of one space and time.
3   Therefore, space and time are intuitions and not general representations or concepts.

Kant discloses three things in this argument that are relevant to our question. First, he tells us that space cannot be constructed out of a set of relations without illicitly assuming spatial regions as their relata. Thus space is a particular and not a common relational property. Secondly, regions of space are a kind of object and not a kind of term. And, finally, nothing in the Argument from Volumes shows that space is the only kind of intuition possible. It provides us at most with *one* way in which the distinction between particulars and common properties can be made.

The Argument from Incongruous Counterparts reinforces all of this. I abbreviate that argument as follows:

1   One body is the incongruent counterpart of the other just in case both have the same properties but cannot simultaneously occupy the same area.[62]
2   There are cases of bodies which have all of their properties in common but still do not occupy the same spatial volume.
3   Therefore, numerical diversity cannot be reconstructed by sets of properties all of which each of the numerically diverse objects has in common with the other.

Here, again, we have an argument purporting to show that there is an indissoluble difference between concepts and intuitions. That difference is guaranteed by the existence of objects which cannot be merely bundles of properties. If the argument is cogent, there must be in any such bundle an ultimate surd that is not itself a property or set of properties. In this case it is a spatial region. And in virtue of this fact anything which is presented to us spatially must also be a particular and not a common relational property.

But we can go further. Both of these arguments allow us to generalize what they illustrate. In the first place, intuitions are not merely linguistic entities. Secondly, they are what I have called particulars rather than individuals. Anything that can be denoted by a definite description can count as an individual. But, as we already know, concepts can be denoted by definite descriptions. This does not, however, transform them into particulars. Thirdly, the only adequate linguistic representation of an intuition is either a logically proper name or the quantifiers in predicate logic together with a uniqueness clause.[63] What Kant calls a spatial region may have properties in common with other spatial regions. It may even be the case that such regions necessarily have some properties or other in common with other spatial regions. But it does not follow that spatial regions themselves *are* such properties. Thus when we denote what has properties in spatial or spatial relations, we single out something that is not itself a property or a set of properties.[64] That is the sense of a Kantian intuition.

NOTES

1   J. Hutchison Stirling, *Textbook to Kant* (Edinburgh: Oliver and Boyd, Tweedale Court, 1881), p. 138.

2   Ibid.

3   Ibid., p. 170n.

4   Ibid.

5   Ibid., p. 52.

6   Edward Caird, *The Critical Philosophy of Immanuel Kant* (Glasgow: James Maclehose, 1909), vol. 1, x. Cf. ibid., p. 266.

7   Ibid. Cf. John Watson, *The Philosophy of Kant Explained* (Glasgow: James Maclehose, 1908), pp. 75 ff., for yet another example of the dangerous confusion of intuition with perception.

8   Stephen Körner, *Kant* (Harmondsworth, England: Penguin, 1955), p. 80. Körner does, to be sure, qualify this by saying that "intuition" covers both perception and what corresponds to it and that "perception" is used in the sense of "empirical perception." Neither qualification alters the semantical situation. The first does not because it merely records the act-object distinction, which is an issue independent of whether intuition should be equated with perception. The second qualification is irrelevant for my present purpose because the whole issue of the propriety of translating *Anschauung* as "perception" can be raised all over again within the context of empirical perception. Cf. T. D. Weldon, *Kant's "Critique of Pure Reason"* (Oxford: Clarendon Press, 1958), p. 110, for another example of the same gloss. More recently, T. E. Wilkerson, *Kant's Critique of Pure Reason* (Oxford: Clarendon Press, 1976), pp. 15-16, follows him in this. Most of this tradition is to be traced to H. J. Paton, *Kant's Metaphysic of Experience* (London: George Allen & Unwin, 1951), vol. 1, p. 95.

9   T. D. Weldon, *op. cit.,* p. 110 and esp. p. 126.

10   A. C. Ewing, *A Short Commentary on Kant's "Critique of Pure Reason"* (Chicago: University of Chicago Press, 1974), pp. 17-18, defends the distinction between intuition and perception by saying that perception is a narrower notion than intuition because there might be beings that intuit by means other than perception. He is right but for the wrong reasons. Other forms of intuition are possible. But that we might acquire those different forms of intuition does not imply anything about the intuition-perception distinction. It implies only that we would perceive in a different way.

11   Immanuel Kant, *Kritik der reinen Vernunft,* A374, A20-B34, A42-B60, B147, A166-B207, A167-B209. In what follows I cite the *Kritik* from the Norman Kemp Smith translation. All citations from other works of Kant are from *Kant's gesammelte Schriften,* the Royal Prussian Academy of Sciences (Berlin: Druck und Verlag von Georg Reimer, 1910). I cite only the relevant work, the volume number, and the page number in such cases. The translations are mine.

12   A166-B207, B147, A166-B207, B160.

13   A166-B207, B147.

14   A20-B34.

15   A166-B207. Cf. *supra,* footnote 11.

16   A42-B60, A167-B209.

17   *De Mundi Sensibilis atque Intelligibilis Forma et Principiis,* vol. 2, para. 10 (italics in text). Hereinafter I refer to this work simply as the *Inaugural Dissertation.*

18   *Inaugural Dissertation,* 2, para. 12 (italics in text).

19   *Logik,* 9, para. 1, note 2.

20   Ibid. Cf. *Logik,* 9, para 2, *passim.*

21   A19.

22   A19. (Italics in text). Cf. *Prolegomena,* 4, para. 8.

23   *Logik,* Introduction, 9, para. 12. Cf. the *Preisschrift über die Fortschritte der Metaphysik,* 20, p. 325 and p. 366.

24   *Logik,* chap. 1, 9, para. 1. Cf. *Inaugural Dissertation,* 2, para. 1 and para. 12.

25   I cannot botanize the flora of the linguistic usage that the expression "concept" has experienced in the course of its chequered history. I understand by "concept" merely what is predicable of many.

26   *Logik,* 9, para. 1, note 2.

27   Cf. Bertrand Russell, *Mysticism and Logic* (Garden City, N.Y.: Doubleday Anchor, n.d.), pp. 202ff. *The Problems of Philosophy* (London: Oxford University Press, 1959), chap. 5, *passim,* for the origins of this distinction.

28   Bertrand Russell, *The Problems of Philosophy* (London: Oxford University Press, 1959), p. 46.

29   Ibid.

30   Russell himself recognizes this in his *Mysticism and Logic,* p. 205.

31   A719-B747. Cf. A19-B33, A50-B74, B146, B158, and A709-B730.

32.   *Logik,* 9, Introduction, para. 4.

33   Thus Meister Eckhart, *Die deutschen Werke,* Josef Quint, ed. (Stuttgart: W. Kohl-hammer Verlag, 1958), vol. 1, Sermon 23, p. 397: "Nû merket! Sant Paulus sprichet: als wir mit enbloeztem antlütz aneschouwen den glanz und die klarheit gotes, sô werden wir weitergebildet und ingebildet in daz bilde, daz als ein bilde ist gotes und der gotheit." Cf. Friedrich Kluge, *Etymologisches Wörterbuch der deutschen Sprache* (Berlin: Walter de Gruyter, 1957), under the entry for the etymology of *Anschauen.*

34   CF. Johann Christoph Adelung, *Versuch eines vollständigen grammatischkritischen Wörterbuchs der hochdeutschen Mundart* (Leipzig: Bernhard Christoph Breitkopf, 1774), under the entry for *Anschauen.*

35   Ibid.

36   Jacob and Wilhelm Grimm, *Deutsches Wörterbuch* (Leipzig: S. Hirtel, 1854), under the entry for *Anschauen.* Cf. Rudolph Christof Eucken, *Geschichte der philosophischen Terminologie* (Leipzig: Veit and Co., 1879), pp. 139 and 149, for the same complaint.

37   Jaakko Hintikka, "On Kant's Notion of Intuition (Anschauung)," in *The First Critique,* Terence Penelhum and J. J. MacIntosh, eds. (Belmont, Calif.: Wadsworth, 1969), pp. 40ff., where he argues that the ordinary use of the term fluctuates. The examples of fluctuation—to continue Hintikka's simile—are, however, ripples on the waters of a continuous stream. Cf. Moltke S. Gram and Richard M. Martin, "The Perils of Plenitude," *Journal of the History of Ideas,* 41 (1980), pp. 497ff. Hintikka and others have discussed the problem of Kantian intuition differently from the way in which I believe it should be debated. Hintikka, *op. cit.,* pp. 40ff., reminds us that a Kantian intuition is a way of referring to an object which is immediate as opposed to reference by means of what that object has in common with other objects, goes on to say that it is a particular rather than a general representation, and concludes by arguing that what Hintikka calls intuitivity is logically distinct from the structure of our sensibility. Charles Parsons joins the debate in his "Kant's Philosophy of Arithmetic," in *Philosophy, Science, and Method,"* S. Morgenbesser, P. Suppes, and M. White, eds. (New York: St. Martin's, 1969), p. 569, by maintaining against Hintikka that the singularity condition of intuitivity is independent of the immediacy condition. And he, unlike Hintikka, argues that there is a more-than-contingent relation between intuitions and sensibility. Manley Thompson, "Singular Terms and Intuitions in Kant's Epistemology," *Review of Metaphysics,* 26 (1972), pp. 314ff., tries to resolve the dispute by arguing that an intuitive representation has no place in language at all. His argument: As soon as we try to represent an intuition as "a whatever," any such phrase applies to the object of any intuition and thereby becomes a general representation. Each of these moves inadequately resolves the problem besetting Kantian intuitions. Take them in turn. Hintikka's claim that Kant can specify what an intuition is without reference to the characteristics of sensibility may be

true. But it still does not tell what it is that is being separated from sensibility. Parsons' claim that the singularity and uniqueness criteria are independent of each other breaks down on the fact that both uniqueness and singularity can be predicated of concepts and intuitions alike. It may be the case that what distinguishes a concept from an intuition is that it is unique but not singular in that it, unlike an intuition, can stand for many. But this still does not prevent an intuition from being a concept that can stand for only one thing. Thompson sees all of this clearly; but he does not get at what I believe to be the fundamental issue; the issue, namely, of what it is to be an extra-linguistic entity satisfying the predicate, ". . . is an intuition."

38   Alexander Gottlieb Baumgarten, *Metaphysica* (Halle: C. H. Hemmerde, 1757), reprinted in the *Akademie-Ausgabe,* 17, p. 104, paras. 347, 620. Jacob Georg Hamann, *Schriften,* Friedrich Roth, ed. (Leipzig: Reimer, 1825), vol. 7, *passim,* hotly and fruitlessly disputes Kant's use of *Anschauung* in his *Metakritik über den Purismum der reinen Vernunft.* Claiming that the concept-intuition distinction is purely linguistic, Hamann argues that a word is used aesthetically when we concentrate on mere printables or vocables. Words then belong to intuition. If you consider them according to their use (*nach dem Geist ihrer Entstehung und Bedeutung*), they are concepts. Hamann's conclusion: Kant falsifies the concept-intuition distinction by failing to locate it in language. Rejoinder: Our very ability to be acquainted aesthetically with words *assumes* that we have the capacity to intuit. It cannot, therefore, be used to tell us what that capacity is.

Johann Gottfried von Herder, *Sämmtliche Werke,* Bernhard Suphan (Berlin: Weidmannsche Buchhandlung, 1881), vol. 21, *passim,* prolongs this farcical spectacle by claiming in his *Eine Metakritik zur Kritik der reinen Vernunft* that Kant confounds sensation with intuition just because he violates ordinary linguistic usage. Received usage, Herder tells us, requires that whatever affects the sensibility be a sensation. This differs from intuition, which is properly applied only to the *perception* or, as Herder quaintly puts it, the perceiving or sensing (*Innewerden*) of sensations. Rejoinder: Sensing for Kant *assumes* intuition; hence, one cannot be conflated with the other. One can only look with charitable pity upon such ludicrous incursions into the Republic of Letters!

Arthur Schopenhauer gives us in his *Die Welt als Wille und Vorstellung, Sämtliche Werke,* Wolfgang Frhr. von Löhneysen, ed. (Frankfurt am Main: Cotta-Insel Verlag, 1960), vol. 1, pp. 592ff., a more serious but no less objectionable account of a Kantian intuition. His contention is basically this: Kant brings thought into intuition and intuition into thought. Thus the concept-intuition distinction collapses. Kant, we are told, brings thought into intuition because he holds that intuition is entirely passive and, further, that an object properly so called is grasped only by the introduction of the categories. But the object of thought is a single, real object. Here Kant allegedly brings intuition into thought. Schopenhauer's objection is completely misdirected because it feeds on an ambiguity in the use of "object." There is a sense in which an object is anything that can perceptually entertain. But there is another sense of that term according to which an object is a composite of what he perceptually entertains after it has been subsumed under the categories. There are, to put it bluntly, nonconceptual awarenesses. Thus Kant does not bring intuition into thought or thought into intuition save in those cases where the second sense of "object" is involved. The concept-intuition distinction, however elusive it may be on other grounds, does not fall prey to this criticism. Cf. Hans Vaihinger, *Commentar zu Kant's "Kritik der reinen Vernunft"* (Stuttgart: Union deutsche Verlagsgesellschaft, 1892), vol. 2, p. 4.

39 Ibid., pp. 56-58, paras. 148-54.

40 Christian August Crusius, *Weg zur Gewissheit und Zuverlässigkeit der menschlichen Erkenntnis* (Leipzig: Johann Friedrich Gleditsch, 1747), para. 119.

41 Georg Friedrich Meier, *Auszug aus der Vernunftlehre* (Halle: Justinus Gebauer, 1752), para. 201. Cf. para. 319.

42 Christian Wolff, *Vernünftige Gedanken von Gott, der Welt, und der Seele des Menschen* (Halle: die Rengerische Buchhandlung, 1770), para. 316.

43 Representative of this tradition are Johann G. Buhle, *Einleitung in die allgemeine Logik und die Kritik der reinen Vernunft* (Göttingen: Vandenhoeck und Ruprecht, 1795), para. 19, *passim;* M. G. Goess, *Systematische Darstellung der Kantischen Vernunftkritik* (Nürnberg: Felsecker, 1794), para. 5; Georg Mellin *Encyclopädisches Wörterbuch der kritischen Philosophie* (Zullichau and Leipzig: F. Frommann, 1797), pp. 167ff.; and Carl C. E. Schmid, *Wörterbuch zum leichteren Gebrauch der Kantischen Schriften* (Jena: Cröter, 1798), pp. 55ff. Mellin gives us this illustration of an intuition. I can cognize (*erkennen*), say, the city of Magdeburg in any of three ways. I can cognize the city by acquiring a set of characteristics (*Merkmale*) from reports of others. I might construct images of the city in my imagination (*Phantasie*). Or, finally, I might intuit (*anschauen*) the city. Suppose, first of all, that I construct a set of characteristics belonging to Magdeburg; namely, that it lies on the western bank of the Elbe, that it is half as wide as it is long, that it has a wide street running through the entire town which divides it into two parts, and that it is bound on either end by a tower. This kind of knowledge assumes the comprehension of such concepts as "bank," "width," and "length."

Yet I can cognize Magdeburg if I have an image, say, of the noonday view of Magdeburg or the length and width of that city. Mellin calls this imaginative representation, which he sharply distinguishes, along with its predecessor, from intuitive awareness. But neither cognition by concepts nor by imagination is a cast of intuition cognition. When I intuit Magdeburg, the distinction between representation (*Vorstellung*) and object (*Gegenstand*) collapses. Here there is not difference between the city of Magdeburg and my cognizance of Magdeburg. I do not need an epistemic instrument — be it concept or image — to which the object supposedly corresponds. Here the city is present to me without any mediation. Thus Mellin explains the requirement of immediacy which Kant himself lays down. He uses the same example to explicate the requirement of uniqueness: No contemplation of concepts can give me the object to which the name "Magdeburg" applies, however detailed the set of concepts is. More than one city can satisfy the description.

Mellin's point is this. You cannot account for an intuition by appealing to entities like concepts which may apply to an object but which cannot replace that object. Nor can you accomplish this feat by supplying an image of the object you want to intuit because the same problem of the relation between the concepts we have which we can correctly apply to that city and the *real* city to which we can apply them arises all over again with respect to the *imaginary* city. All of this is true. But it is also just where Mellin's explication founders. We can be immediately acquainted with concepts just as we can be immediately acquainted with the objects that fall under them. And conceptual objects of immediate acquaintance can be just as unique as what is given to us in intuition, which is not conceptual. The immediacy and uniqueness requirements which Mellin's Magdeburg example illustrate serve only to tell us something true about intuitions. They do not tell us what an intuition is.

Wilfrid Sellars, *Science and Metaphysics* (New York: Humanities Press, 1968), pp. 3ff., presents the Mellin example in contemporary clothing. Sellars reasons as follows. We must describe an intuition of a cube, say, as "this-cube" (a representation of a this-such). Whenever we exclaim "this-cube," "cube" does not occur as a general representation. Sellar's reason is that "this-cube" is what he calls conceptually prior to the occurrence of "cube" in a judgment. "This-cube" is just the representation of what Sellars calls a this-such. This does not involve predication; therefore, it is non-judgmental. And so, the distinction between intuitions and concepts is preserved. Thus Sellars.

True, but useless. Suppose that we try to separate intuitions from concepts by saying, as Sellars does, that the semantical reflection of our acquaintance with any Kantian intuition can be described in a nonjudgmental way. We can say that same thing about any Kantian concept. And even if we waive this otherwise lethal objection, the Sellarsian position fares no better. We can ask about the relation between a Sellarsian "this" and a Sellarsian "such" in an intuition. But this is just the problem which faces any attempt to explicate the concept-intuition distinction from the very outset. The issue which the Sellarsian gloss leaves inviolate is what the relation of our knowledge of a such is to our knowledge of a this. That is just where we came in.

44   Buhle, *op cit.*, pp. 63-64; J. G. C. Kiesewetter, *Versuch einer fasslichen Darstellung der wichtigsten Wahrheiten der kritischen Philosophie für Uneingeweihte* (Berlin: Wilhelm Oemigke der Jüngere, 1803), pp. 39ff.; and Georg Andreas Will, *Vorlesungen über die Kantische Philosophie* (Altdorf: im Monatischen Verlag, 1788), para. 2, *passim.*

45   M. G. Goess, *op. cit.*, para. 15 and para. 19.

46   Jacobus Zallinger, *Disquisitionum Philosophicae Kantianae* (Riga: Vandelicus, 1799), vol. 2, pp. 51-52.

47   Mellin, *op. cit.*, pp. 260ff., mentions but does not endorse this view.

48   This account is set forth by Johann G. Buhle, *op. cit.*, pp. 63-64. It is, however, expressly denied by J. G. C. Kiesewetter, *op. cit.*, pp. 39ff., and Georg Andreas Will, *Vorlesungen über die Kantische Philosophie* (Altdorf: im Monatischen Verlag, 1788), para. 2, *passim.* Cf. Richard Smyth, *Forms of Intuition* (The Hague: Martinus Nyhoff, 1978), pp. 139ff., for a transcription of this hermeneutical distress. Cf. Kant, Academy edition, 2, pp. 387 and 397; 24, pp. 25ff.; 20, p. 325; *Logik,* para. 21; *Reflection* 2392; A69-B94, A117-B118.

49   Cf. *supra,* footnote 25.

50   Cf. Rudolf Carnap, *Meaning and Necessity* (Chicago: University of Chicago Press, 1956), pp. 32ff. He prefaces this introduction by defining "concept" as what is expressed in a language as a designator for properties, relations, and the like. He then says that a concept is also a property which is objectively possessed by whatever has it. He then introduces individual expressions. And then we are supposed to derive the notion of an individual concept as the intension of an individual expression. I provisionally adopt this account of individual concepts, not because I think the Carnapian formulation to be adequate, but merely because the account as it stands is free from contradiction. It allows us to *talk* about concepts without entangling ourselves in the consequence that a predicate can never be the subject of a proposition. None of this helps in deciding whether there *are* such entities as individual concepts.

51   *Welches sind die wirklichen Fortschritte, die die Metaphysik seit Leibnizens und Wolffs Zeiten in Deutschland gemacht hat?* 20, p. 325. Cf. also, 20, p. 266, where *Erkenntnis* is called a judgment.

52   A320-B377

53   *Inaugural Dissertation,* paras. 1, 12.

54   Cf. Richard Smyth, *op. cit.,* pp. 159ff., for a largely unsuccessful attempt to up-hold this view. Cf. Ralph Walker, *Kant* (London: Routledge & Kegan Paul, 1978), pp. 42-43, for a similar account.

55   A166-B208. Cf. *Prolegomena,* paras. 24, 26. The distinction between an intuition and a sensation is confirmed by what Kant says elsewhere. In his *Reflexionen zur Metaphysik,* 17, p. 658, he separates intuition from sensation in experience and, again, 17, p. 662, where he repeats the distinction. Carl C. E. Schmid, *Critik der reinen Vernunft im Grundrisse* (Jena: in der Cröckerschen Buchhandlung, 1794), pp. 12-13, gives contemporary confirmation of this:

> Jede Vorstellung ist an sich eine Modification des Gemüths. Sofern sie bloss auf das Subject der Vorstellungsfähigkeit bezogen wird, heisst sie nur Empfindung; sie wird Erkenntnis, wenn die Beziehung auf einen blossen d. i. von aller Vorstellung unterschiedenen Gegenstand hinzukommt. Diese Beziehung kann entweder unmittelbar geschehen, oder mittelbar durch Merkmale, die mehrern Gegenständen gemein sein können. Im ersten Fall ensteht die Vorstellung eines einzelnen Gegenstandes, die durch ihn allein möglich ist, Anschauung; im anderen eine allgemeine Vorstellung durch (ver-bundene) Merkmale, Begriff.

56   A20-B34. Cf. A52-B60, B147, A166-B207, and A374.

57   Cf. A19-B34.

58   *Prolegomena,* paras. 18, 19, 20, 21, 22, 25.

59   Ibid., para. 19.

60   Cf. my "The Crisis of Syntheticity," *Kant-Studien,* 121 (1980), pp. 172ff., for a discussion of these arguments in another context.

61   A25-B39.

62   Cf. *Von dem ersten Grunde des Unterschiedes der Gegenden im Raume,* 10, pp. 375ff., and *Prolegomena,* 13.

63   I regard this position as conclusive. Others may not. There are three objections to it that are legion in the literature. Some might reject my conclusion because they hold that proper names can be repeatedly applied. And, so the objection goes, this is something they share in common with concepts. The initial claim is true. The conclusion drawn from it is false. The same proper name can admittedly be applied on a variety of occasions — which does not imply that it is incapable of being used to single out one and only one object on each occasion of its use. Others might be tempted to argue that proper names can be eliminated by predicate expressions, thus forcing the assimilation of intuitions to concepts. The objection is

cogent; but it affects only ordinary proper names, not *logically* proper names.

Still others might complain that the account I give here is glaringly defective because it traduces Kant's text. He says, we might be told, that what we are aware of when we think of things not given in intuition is, not an intuition, but a concept. The usual admonitory references are B157, B307, and *Prolegomena*, para. 45. This objection will not do. The passages usually cited to support it assume a sense of "immediacy" according to which anything that is immediate must be a *particular* presented to consciousness noninferentially. But "immediacy" has another sense. Although Kant does not always distinguish it from the first sense, for all the objection shows, it still can be in the text. We might say that *anything*, particular or not, is immediate just insofar as it is present to consciousness noninferentially. The second sense of "immediacy" allows — indeed, demands — the possibility of intuitive awareness of concepts as well as intuitions. *Prolegomena*, para. 8, supports this because the requirement of immediacy is rejected there as necessary for intuitivity.

64   For a partial anticipation of this account, see F. N. Bauer, *Erläuterung und Prüfung des Kantischen Systems* (Gotha: Carl Wilhelm Ettinger, 1794), pp. 22-23. Ralph Walker, *op. cit.,* p. 423 and pp. 60-61, introduces the notion of a proper name only to say, regrettably, that it represents individual concepts.

Wille and *Willkür* in
Kant's Theory of Action

Introduction

The only really good advice about translations may indeed be not to rely on them. This is not to say that there are not some good translations of some of Kant's writings but that many others are curiously amiss some of the time when they, often apparently without hesitation or argument, opt for a particular rendering of some crucial terms, thereby coloring in essential regards any understanding to be derived from the translation. Several mutually compatible reasons for going astray may be at work. (1) The translator misses a nuance of (in our case) eighteenth-century German, either ordinary or philosophical. (2) Details of his or her translation are philosophically prejudicial in that they exemplify philosophical beliefs of the translator's period or milieu or else reflect an inadequate grasp of relevant philosophical issues. (3) Philosophical usage has shifted since the date of translation, and the reader understands some details in a fashion not intended by the translator. (Not all of these are of course difficulties just with translation.)

I have set myself the task of trying to make a bit clearer what it is Kant might mean when he uses the terms *Wille, Willkür,* and *willkür-lich.* I initially became interested in the question of their translation

Ralf Meerbote is associate professor of philosophy, University of Rochester, Rochester, New York.

when I noticed that the last of the three is often translated as "arbitrary" (and as "arbitrarily" in its adverbial use). Such a translation seems wrong on many occasions and highly misleading on others. It ought to be possible to translate better by considering *willkürlich* together with its noun cognate *Willkür* and the latter, in turn, in connection with Kant's characterization of *Wille*.

In the first part of these remarks I shall give an extremely brief sketch, relatively independent of exegetical details, of what I take the work to be which Kant assigns to both *Wille* and *Willkür* in his theory of action, including cognitive action. In part 2, I continue this discussion and briefly allude to some passages which support, not always unambiguously, some of what I say in part 1. I shall here also further develop aspects of the theme of moral and of cognitive action which lead to Kant's conception of *a priori* legislative action. *A priori* geometrical cognition will be one interesting example of such action. Kant's conception of *a priori* legislative action and of its circumstances will have consequences for any proper understanding of *Wille, Willkür,* and *willkürlich,* as we shall see. In part 3, I shall provide some details of German eighteenth- and nineteenth-century usage (some of them influenced by Kant's own substantive positions). In part 4, I catalog what standard Anglo-Saxon translators have come up with by way of translations of the terms under discussion here and, finally, in part 5, I make some recommendations as to good translation. Coming after the first four parts of my presentation, the recommendations will be rather obvious and of interest only because they fail to agree with a good deal of what was cataloged in part 4.

1   *Kant on Mental Action*

In his *Critique of Judgment,* section 10, and elsewhere, Kant accepts what has now become the well-known pro-attitude — belief model of human agency. At least typical cases of human agency are cases of acting based on a practical reason. Such cases Kant describes as cases of spontaneous acting and of acting by means of *Willkür,* and the requirement that such acting be based on reasons is explained by means of the pro-attitude — belief model, roughly as follows. Some person P has a pro-attitude toward achieving H and believes that performing G will (or will likely) have the consequence of achieving H (or contribute toward such an achievement). The conjunction of his pro-attitude and of this belief constitutes P's practical reason R for performing G. (Additional conditions may have to be satisfied in order for P to act on R.)

All spontaneous human action based on practical reasons is mental action, a point I shall not elaborate on here except to say that mental action is to be distinguished from bodily (physical) processes and events (under physicalist descriptions) but, according to Kant, not distinguished in a way that makes for a substance-dualism of the mental and the physical. Persons make choices among alternative actions available to them, and *Willkür,* in its most generic conception, is the capacity to choose on the basis of desires. Animals and human beings alike possess *Willkür* understood in this fashion, but only the *Willkür* of the latter can fail to be pathologically (i.e., sensibly) necessitated and hence can be spontaneous and *arbitrium liberum.*[1]   The pro-attitude—belief model has the obvious consequence that mental states taking propositional objects need to be ascribed to human beings, and it is conceivable that Kant—disregarding the problem of animals—for this reason alone thinks that human beings typically act spontaneously by means of *Willkür.* I am at any rate ascribing to him the position that for human beings or persons to act spontaneously based on practical reasons is for them to act in a manner essentially requiring choice involving propositional pro-attitudes and beliefs in means-end relations. Hence choice is here determined (governed) by beliefs in means-end relations, the ends introduced as objects of antecedent pro-attitudes. I take this to be a faithful elaboration of Kant's claim that spontaneous human agency is agency under maxims, prescriptions, rules, or interest.[2]

This account has the consequence that *Willkür* is here determined (governed) by practical reasons in the spirit of our model. If human *Willkür* is the capacity to choose, based on desires, in a manner waiting to be representationally determined (governed), then what is human *Wille?* *P*'s practical reason for acting one way rather than another is constituted by the above conjunction of beliefs and pro-attitudes, and Kant in his later writings can more often than not be found saying that it is *Wille* which determines choice, or, more typically, that it is *Wille* which determines the power of choice or *Willkür* (for human beings). This ought, then, to mean that *Wille* is practical reason as just explained.[3] More precisely, *Wille* is the conjunction of beliefs concerning means-end relations and of pro-attitudes described as pro-attitudes toward ends standing in such believed-in relations (and such ends typically themselves potentially objects of pro-attitudes because further represented or representable as means toward other ends). Hence there typically will be in this fashion representationally brought about pro-attitudes. *Wille* and *Willkür* are in this manner closely intertwined.

But it turns out that there is a complication which needs to be taken into account since it has consequences for any proper understanding of the terms under discussion here. The conjunctive character of *Wille,* or practical reason as just explained, means that *Wille* is of the character both of beliefs in means-end relations and of pro-attitudes properly connected, but Kant, within the model of acting on practical reasons which I have ascribed to him, differentiates between heteronomous and autonomous acting, and the difference seems to touch both on the nature of the determination by appropriate means-end relations and on the conditions under which appropriate pro-attitudes arise in the mental life of persons.[4]

In cases of heteronomous (but still spontaneous) acting, the belief in question is one of an empirical-consequence relation, typically described by Kant as requiring an empirical theoretical principle,[5] and the relevant pro-attitudes arise in a manner somehow expressive of a person's contingent mental life. Both parts of this description make for heteronomy of heteronomous acting. It is natural to describe this by saying that practical reason here is empirical practical reason.[6] Consonant with certain other terminological practices of Kant's, we could also say that the beliefs and pro-attitudes in question are here empirically gained and developed. Empirical practical reason here is *Wille* in its empirical employment. As before, such *Wille* determines *Willkür.*

Wanting to lunch in pleasant company, I direct my steps toward the faculty club, since I believe that doing so will bring me nearer desirable company. My belief is of an empirical consequence-relation, and wanting to lunch in the described fashion is an empirically acquired preference. My belief is based on reasons in a manner which allows me to say that I empirically cognize that quite likely, if I go to the club, I shall lunch in pleasant company. At the same time, lunching in pleasant company can be correctly believed by me to be a means toward yet further ends, such as finding out what the dean is up to at this time (perhaps because pleasant company there tends to be informed about such things). Both the fact that I can here empirically cognize means-end relations and the fact that a cognitive action of mine (finding out about the dean) can itself be a desired end indicate the close connections between conditions of empirical cognition and our model of acting based on practical reason. On one hand, my relevant beliefs, constituting part of my practical reason, are themselves such that their objects are subject to empirical theoretical determination, with the result that in this fashion theoretical reasons can be part of my practical reason. Part of my practical reason consists here of a belief based on empirical theoretical reasons-connections. And on the other hand, cognitive actions are themselves such that they can be ends related to empirical practical reasons in that my wish to be informed is part of my practical reason for going to the club.

Suppose I wish to cognize whether p is true, and suppose I believe that if I (i) cognize whether e is true (for some "e"), (ii) cognize whether e is good evidence for "p," and (iii) believe that p based on (i) and (ii), then I cognize whether p is true. I then have a practical reason for satisfying (i)-(iii). But it can now also be asked whether I cognize the conditional connection between (i)-(iii) on the one hand and cognize whether p on the other, and if so, how I cognize this connection. Part of Kant's answer to this most recent question consists of saying that my belief in the connection is no longer based on empirical theoretical reasons but on *a priori* ones. In particular this is true of what he (in the cases he is interested in) takes to be a consequence of (ii) taken by itself, to wit, my cognizing whether there are causal connections between the truths of "e" and "p." It is in regard to this most recent question that he speaks of *a priori* (theoretical) determination or *a priori* legislation, i.e., a believing based on *a priori* legislation rather than empirical determination. With such a result, we have, according to Kant, reached a species of cognizing which helps make for autonomy of some aspects of mental life. Some of the conditions of the possibility of empirical cognition are not themselves equivalent or reducible to empirically cognizable states of affairs, and what is empirically cognizable does not justify belief in such conditions[7] (Kantian positions I shall put to use in part 2). Notice that all of this is compatible with my having a practical reason for cognizing whether e is good evidence for "p," or, for that matter, for cognizing that if (i)-(iii) (or even only if I cognize that there are causal connections), then I will (or this will contribute toward the state of affairs when I) cognize that p. I may, for example, believe that if I cognize any of the latter matters, this will contribute toward my understanding of the nature of cognition (an understanding I wish to attain). *A priori* legislation or determination is typically thought of by Kant as being of pure (nonempirical) nature. For our model here, this suggests that descriptions which make for autonomy of aspects of mental life relevant here are descriptions of a pure practical reason at work.

According to Kant, the following is a further important feature of our belief—pro-attitude model of acting based on practical reason.

Not every end is a means toward a further end. Kant, even with his four-to-five-hour lunches in pleasant and informed company, did not think that good lunching is an end but not a means, or an end in itself. But according to him there are such ends, that of acting morally the most plausible or prominent among them.[8] Now notice that if acting morally serves no further purpose, then our model has us say that, although I may have a practical reason for so acting in the case at hand, I have no further practical reason for being moral. The pro-attitude in question (wanting to act morally) is an aspect of our mental life somehow fundamentally different from those aspects which arise in the contingent course of such a life. That there are pro-attitudes like wanting to be moral is another feature which has Kant speak of autonomy of parts of mental life.

Notice that even if we say that acting morally serves no further purpose, it still will be the case that acting in such a manner as to satisfy the categorical imperative is to act in a manner believed to have the consequence of acting morally. For example, that will be the case if we think of acting in accordance with such an imperative as a means toward achieving the end of being moral rather than as being conceptually identical with being moral. Thought of in this manner, obeying the categorical imperative does serve a further purpose. Similarly, it may turn out that looking for causes serves the purpose of empirically cognizing. What is of interest to us here in all of this is that if I am right about some such overall characterization of ends-in-themselves, then there will be pro-attitudes and hence spontaneous mental states or actions which do not arise or occur for further practical reasons, a result which I also shall return to in part 2. Not even pure practical reason would induce (in the spirit of further practical reasons) such attitudes (but, as indicated above, it would be at work in *a priori* legislation of means-end connections like those of the categorical imperative). If even such attitudes are of *Willkür* (as they are according to Kant), we would have reached with them cases of *Willkür* not determined, i.e., themselves brought about by *Wille* (but furthered by *Wille* in the sense of *Wille* being practical reason for taking steps believed to lead to the satisfaction of the attitude).[9]

To be acting *willkürlich* is to be acting by means of *Willkür*, and this must now be understood in full view of the doctrines of *Wille* and *Willkür* just sketched.

2 *Some Passages, Textual Complications, and What It Can Take to be*
Willkürlich

Kant's discussions of the conditions of human spontaneous action
based on reasons are scattered through a number of his writings, including (in addition to the *Critique of Judgment* and its two Introduc-
tions) the *Critique of Pure Reason,* [10] the *Critique of Practical Reason,* [11] the
Groundwork of the Metaphysics of Morals, [12] the *Metaphysics of Morals,* [13]
and *Religion Within the Limits of Reason Alone.* [14] All but the *Critique of
Pure Reason* and the *Critique of Judgment* discuss various conditions of
such action, almost invariably with particular reference to the moral-
ity of human actions, an emphasis usually shared by the Kant literature. Most of what Kant has to say in these works supports the sketch
given by me in part 1. In particular, the preface and section 3 of the
Groundwork[15] introduce three general species of determination of
choice, namely, by motives of the senses (such as for animals), by
motives of the understanding (such as in heteronomous spontaneous
action?), and by motives of ideas and of pure reason (such as in
autonomous, *a priori* legislative, spontaneous action). A typical theme
is that *Willkür* chooses actions and *Wille* determines such choice.

At the same time it is fairly clear that Kant's own conception of the
differences and relations between *Wille* and *Willkür* did not remain
static and that it, terminologically at least, developed only gradually
into an unambiguous statement of the views outlined in part 1.[16]
But even the relatively early writings such as the *Critique of Pure Reason,*
with its reference to spontaneity and to geometrical synthesis due to
Willkür,[17] seem to me already to contain *in essence* the mature view,
even if not fully stated and even though, specifically, *Wille* is not yet
clearly differentiated from *Willkür.*

A number of issues inextricably involved in the development of
Kant's thoughts on these matters complicate both his and our understanding of the issue. I shall mention only the following (and then
promptly set them aside). (1) There is the problem of how to fit in
his various notions of freedom, such as freedom negatively and freedom positively conceived. The mature view is that spontaneous
Willkür is freedom negatively conceived and is not what others may
think of as free will. Free will, according to Kant, turns out to be
freedom positively conceived, or autonomy. (2) There is the problem
of how to distinguish precisely between intending, choosing our action,
and acting. *Willkür* is to choose between alternative actions, and
Wille is to determine choice and hence "not directly" action. But it
seems to me that Kant does not furnish precise relevant distinctions.

(3) Sometimes *Willkür* is simply the power to desire or choose, at other times such a power specifically as determined by practical reason (by *Wille* in either its empirical or its pure employment). As I already indicated,[18] Kant in some fundamental respects fails to explain choosing altogether. (4) Kant is not at all precise in distinguishing among powers, dispositions, actions, and events, a fact which makes some of his doctrines more obscure than they otherwise would be.[19]

I now turn specifically to a discussion of Kant's use of both the adjective and the adverb *willkürlich*. The generic sense of the term is that of "being based on *Willkür*" and hence it modifies mental actions. I said earlier that such action is to be distinguished from bodily movement under physicalist descriptions, and it can be argued[20] that Kant holds that mental actions under proper mentalist descriptions do not stand under the conditions of strict causal determinism laid down in the Second Analogy of the *Critique of Pure Reason*. This allows saying that there is a way of conceiving of mental actions such that they are not explained causally but *without* thereby *violating* causal laws.[21] But at the same time the temptation to confuse "under a description not explained by causal laws" with "violates causal laws" may explain the common tendency to think of mental actions as, first, not being lawful (in any sense of law) and, second, as we shall see, arbitrary because not causally governed under one description. The temptation should be resisted. For the purposes of this paper, acting based on practical reasons is of central importance, and in this regard, an action which is *willkürlich* is precisely an action determined by practical reason.

At the same time, Kant's views concerning *a priori* legislative action (in either moral or epistemic contexts) throw additional light on a temptation to consider at least such (autonomous) actions as *willkürlich* in a respect somehow making for arbitrariness. (Such actions are therefore also important for the purposes of this paper.) Two considerations need to be kept apart here. (A) Relevant means-end relations are, due to *a priori* legislative action, believed in in a fashion which is incompatible with saying that the belief is a cognition, at least of the variety which Kant labels "empirical cognition." For example, to believe that satisfying certain epistemic conditions leads to cognizing empirically is not to cognize empirically. There is no empirical theoretical determination forthcoming of *such* means-end connections, and Kant can be found to describe the possession of (doxastic attitudes toward) principles expressing such connections as originary. Although we here have practical reasons for acting so as to satisfy the means (and maybe even for the *a priori* legislating), the belief in question is not supported by theoretical determinations (of a certain sort).[22] But the absence of theoretical determinations (of a sort), or the originary character of relevant beliefs, may lead to the suggestion that *arbitrary beliefs* are being held here (and hence that we are dealing here with mental actions standing in crucial respects under no non-arbitrary conditions). (B) Since being moral serves no further purpose,[23] we have already seen that wanting to be moral (a pro-attitude) is given in some fundamental way which cannot itself be explained by means of (possession of a) further practical reason. Only means in a believed-in means-end connection toward further ends can be explained in this fashion. In this sense there is no practical reason for wanting to be moral. Not even pure practical reason can in this sense bring about the pro-attitude (but, as we have seen, pure practical reason will be at work when it comes to satisfying the pro-attitude).

In (A) there was an absence of a theoretical determination (of a sort), and in (B) we have an absence of a further practical reason, as just explained. Just as in (A), one may be tempted to hold in (B) that we are dealing with an arbitrariness, since (in (B)) we do not have a further teleologically founded attitude. But I submit that even in (A) and (B) "arbitrary" is mistaken or at best misleading.

I shall say no more about (B) except that Kant does not believe the moral attitude to be arbitrary. But (A) can be further illustrated, I believe, by considering Kant's own discussion of *a priori* geometrical synthesis (presuming at the same time some due allowances for differences in the sorts of *a priori* legislative actions involved here as opposed to the cases of categorial conditions or the categorical imperative). Mathematical synthesis,[24] so we are told by Kant,[25] is *willkürlich,* and analysis of the details of his explanation[26] reveals that at least one important factor which makes such synthesis *willkürlich* is that it essentially involves an *a priori* originary introduction of a unit of length-measurement (say) subject to *a priori* rules of geometrical determination. The introduction is originary precisely in the sense that metrics are not themselves determined by any description (synthesis) of nonmetrical space. Hence we are dealing here once again with a legislating not itself grounded on antecedent facts of an appropriate sort. Kant's relational analysis of orientation[27] provides another example: Any particular standard of, say, left-handedness needs to be originarily introduced.

But in all such cases it would be improper to conceive of originary legislating as arbitrary if this means *inconsistent, ill-considered, random, or not binding.* I believe that originary legislating should not even be considered as conventional, at least on some interpretations of conventionality. Kant's conception of the nature and role of genius becomes relevant in this context.[28]   It is precisely genius which is to provide rules in originary fashion since it is the mark of works of genius that they are creative. But to say that genius creates or invents rules is not to say that it does so in a fashion making for arbitrariness.

Other examples of Kant's of what is *willkürlich* are given by him in his discussion[29] of what he thinks of as inventively designed signs (such as letters and notes) as opposed to natural signs (such as pulse and smoke). (His view on the former explains why even assignments of nominal definitions to words, and not just mathematical concepts, are regarded by him as *willkürlich*[30]) Again, inventiveness is the mark of what is *willkürlich* here, and the sense of the latter must be understood in the context of Kant's theory of creativity (a task I cannot undertake here).

3   *German Usage During and After Kant's Time*

J. R. Silber has claimed[31] that in Kant both *Wille* and *Willkür* (and their cognates) receive technical meanings not recognized in ordinary German. In ordinary German usage, according to Silver, *Wille* includes both Kant's *Wille* and *Willkür* (as well as *Gesinnung*). But it seems to me that the changes, differences, and correlations among the terms in question in the eighteenth century and later (partly due to Kant's own influence) are both more bewildering and suggestive than Silber allows. I shall make my case by considering relevant entries in Adelung,[32] Sanders,[33] and Grimm.[34]

According to Adelung, *Wille* in one of its senses is conceived as very broad indeed, as the capacity to want (to act), including acting through precepts. One definition of *Willkür* is that of the capacity to act as one sees fit,[35] a characterization ambiguous both in English and in German. It is also defined as *free choice.* Most interestingly, Adelung adds that "more specifically" *Willkür* is to be *opposed* to *reasoned* choice based on distinct representations. *Willkür* is used here as expressing *censure,* and such a connotation is most characteristically carried over to *willkürlich.* When taken as a term of censure, *capriciousness* would be a good English rendering. But another sense of *willkürlich* distinguished by Adelung is that of *being dependent on the will of a law-giver,* such as in matters of punishment, as opposed to being dependent on "natural" conditions.[36] But it would seem that in such a use, capriciousness or arbitrariness cannot be taken to be built into the sense of the term.

In Sanders, *willkürlich* and *Willkür* as expressive of censure are prominently stressed. To act *willkürlich* is often to act in violation of conditions which ought to determine or limit action.

Grimm's entries are the most detailed (and adduce Kant himself as an authority). *Wille* and *Willkür* are sometimes taken as being in conflict with one another, as in cases where *Wille* enforces what is morally good. Grimm quotes here Goethe's "Vor dem Willen schweigt die Willkür stille." Willing (*Wollen*) in general is power (to act), in contrast to passivity as well as to natural drives (as presumably in Kant's pathological necessitation). (Luther: "Es ist gar viel anderes was du willig tust und was du natürlich tust.") *Willkür* is here often expressive of censure, whereas *Wollen* in general is *"freie Verfügung (arbitrarium)"* or "self-determination."

But Grimm also stresses what he calls Kant's philosophical definitions, and what he says there agrees with what I have said above. *Wille* is practical reason, determining *Willkür*. In their "scientific" sense, Grimm says, *willkürlich* and *Willkür* do *not* express censure as in Fichte's "Es ist kein Wille ohne Willkür." Specifically, *willkürlich* is expressive of intellectual and artistic creativity ("imaginative, ideal, and not real," Grimm says), not itself derivative from the lawfulness of laws of nature. Grimm refers to Kant's views on the nature of language and of mathematical concepts and quotes Goethe's "willkürlich und geschmackvoll." *Willkürlich* also connotes *deliberate* and *conscious* and, interestingly enough, "of physical events *without cognizable ground.*" ("Spontaneous combustion" comes to mind as an example in English of the latter kind.)

For our purposes, the shift away from a conception of *Willkür* and its cognates (as censure-laden) to a more "scientific" conception is the single most important result of this philological-historical survey, since it is this shift which frees Kant's *Wille* to play its role as practical reason determining (more or less successfully) *Willkür* "scientifically" understood. But the fact that such a shift needed to occur also helps us understand the ambiguity in *Willkür,* which so often finds itself expressed in the temptation to conceive of it as arbitrariness (including, prominently, intent to censure), rather than (just) in the spirit of Kant's inventiveness or work of genius, on the one hand, and of his conception of human agency typically based on practical reasons, on the other.

4   *Anglo-Saxon Translators and Present-Day American Usage*

We have seen that there can be mental actions and states involving *Willkür* and not determined by reasons (of various sorts) and others based on reasons (both theoretical and practical), and we also have seen that there is a generic sense of human *Willkür* in which physicalist descriptions are not appropriate to action based on such *Willkür*. None of this has the consequence that *willkürlich* in particular should be translated as *arbitrary* (if the latter means what I suggested it might by enumeration above). That *artibrary* comes from *arbitrium*, which is Kant's Latin for *Willkür*, may of course have suggested to some such a translation.[37]

Obviously, the value of the translation is as much a function of English as it is of German. The most important Anglo-Saxon translators of Kant's writings are as follows in regard to our translation problem. Lewis White Beck[38] distinguishes between *Wille* and *Willkür* by considering the former to be practical reason and the latter the power of choice (awaiting determination by practical reason). T. K. Abbott[39] translates *Wille* as *rational will* and *Willkür* as *elective will*. J. H. Bernard [40] and J. C. Meredith[41] use *will* in crucial passages and, unlike Beck and Abbott, do not seem overly concerned about possible ambiguities. N. K. Smith at B562 translates *Willkür* as *will*. In the second edition of T. M. Greene's and H. H. Hudson's translation of *Religion*, the distinction between *Wille* and *Willkür* is marked by subscripting (*will*$_w$ for *Willkür*).[42]

When we turn to *willkürlich*, we see that the divergences are no less severe. All four translators of the *Critique of Pure Reason*[43] translate *willkürlich* at the crucial passage at B757 by *arbitrary*. A. Wood[44] proceeds in the same fashion. So does M. Gregor.[45] R. Hartman and W. Schwarz[46] in one crucial passage [47] translate (the adverb) as *arbitrarily* [*freely*] but for other passages seem to get tired of this cumbersome procedure and fall back to *arbitrary*. (However, it is fair to assume that they wish this to be understood, at least some of the time, as *arbitrary* [*free*].) Beck, Greene, and Hudson (at least *via* Silber), and apparently Hartman and Schwarz, are aware that *freely* or *voluntary* or *of choice* would be happier translations.

As indicated earlier, what is a good translation is obviously, among other things, a function of the language into which we translate. A glance at American usages [48] supports my earlier contention that *arbitrary* is at best misleading (and often simply false) as a translation of *willkürlich*. (*Will* is similarly inadequate as a translation of *Wille* since it is too imprecise and sometimes covers *Willkür.*) *Arbitrate* means *decide* and *determine* (innocuous enough meanings), but one basic meaning of *arbitrary* is also that of *being fixed or arrived at through will or* [!] *caprice.* Another given meaning, *decisive but unreasoned,* is at best too vague (and sometimes surely wrong for Kant). And it does not need pointing out that other possible connotations, such as *at random* or *without definite aim,* also miss the mark. I think it is fair to say that American usage makes *arbitrary* a poor translation indeed.

5   Recommendations

As promised, these recommendations will be rather obvious, following parts 1-4. Given the history of the terms I chose for discussion here, both during and after Kant's time, given Kant's own progression of gradually unfolding terminological and substantive complexity, and given more or less current American usages, we must find fault with many, but not all, of the translations referred to in part 4. Since Kant's view itself is not unwaveringly the same in all of his writings, at least terminologically, it is at the same time true that no one set of preferred translations may do justice to all relevant passages in his works. But with respect to his mature view, I now make the following suggestions. When Kant discusses nonphysicalist determination of human action, distinguish between $Wille_1$ and $Wille_2$ and translate the former as *empirical practical reason* and the latter as *pure practical reason* and hence *Wille* as *practical reason,* all of this in the spirit of our pro-attitude — belief model. Translate *Willkür* as *power of choice* (from among alternative actions). *Willkür* is determined by $Wille_1$ or $Wille_2$. (ends-in-themselves may pose special problems.)

In light of the mental character of human actions based on *Willkür,* in contexts of an account of such actions translate *willkürlich* as voluntary, of choice, or *willed,* understanding the latter notions in a spirit compatible with our model. For contexts of *a priori* originary legislation, when *willkürlich* is a characterization of what is legislated, translate it as *inventively chosen* or, indeed, *originary.* Terms like *capricious, arbitrary* (given its prominent meaning), and even *willful* should be avoided altogether, unless the translation is of a passage (if such can be found) in which it is evident that Kant is speaking of caprice or randomness. Aside from this, *arbitrary* would (sometimes) be appropriate only if one has it mean strictly *not derivative from antecedent theoretical determinations.*[49] Finally, I ought to note that in present-day ordinary German, *willkürlich* is quite close to *arbitrary,* but we have been interested here in Kant's usage of the term.

NOTES

1 In the *Critique of Pure Reason,* see B561-2. (The first *Critique* will be cited in the usual way. All other references to Kant's writings will be to the Academy edition, abbreviated by "Ac. ed.," followed by the volume number and, when appropriate, the page number.) It is not wholly clear why Kant wants to distinguish in this regard sharply between animals and human beings and at the same time attribute to both some sort of *Willkür* and mental life to the former.

2 See, e.g., the *Groundwork of the Metaphysics of Morals,* Ac. ed., 4, p. 413, and p. 427, and cf. L. W. Beck, *A Commentary on Kant's Critique of Practical Reason* (Chicago, 1960), p. 35. Beck gives further references.

3 This agrees with Beck's results in his *Commentary.* Beck also points out that Kant confuses *Wille* and *Willkür* when he says (sometimes) that reason determines *Wille.*

4 I have explored some of this in a paper for a projected *Festschrift* for L. W. Beck.

5 Cf., e.g., the *First Introduction* to the *Critique of Judgment,* Ac. ed., 20, p. 196.

6 Cf. Beck, *Commentary,* pp. 75-76.

7 The justification provided by transcendental arguments for *a priori* conditions must not be confused with this.

8 I say "most plausible or prominent" because it could be argued that cognizing is, according to Kant, also such an end. It certainly is the case that, in regard to *a priori* legislation, he compares cognizing positively with acting morally. The remaining question would be whether the pro-attitude toward cognizing (not to be confused with believing or with believing with truth) is fundamental in the way in which the attitude toward being moral is.

9 A more careful analysis would have to raise the question whether there is a sense in which pure practical reason motivates after all.

10 Cf. B562.

11 Ac. Ed., 5, pp. 28-29 (and elsewhere).

12 Ac. ed., 4, pp. 446ff. (and elsewhere).

13 See Ac. ed., 6, p. 407.

14 Ac. ed., 6, p. 20ff.

15 Ac. ed., 4, pp. 387-92, 446ff.

16 Cf. J. R. Silber, "The Ethical Significance of Kant's *Religion,*" in T. M. Green and H. H. Hudson's translation of Kant's *Religion* (New York, 1960), esp. 83-84. Beck and T. K. Abbott hold similar views.

17 B757.

18 Cf. fn. 1.

19 Cf. Silber, *op. cit.,* cxivff.

20 I attempt to do so in the paper mentioned in fn. 4.

21 This might be so in the spirit of anomalous monism, referred to in the same paper. I am not claiming, however, that Kant's further distinction between heteronomous and autonomous spontaneous action can easily be fitted into anomalous monism.

22 Cf. fn. 7.

23 I have not attempted to argue for this, but it is clear that Kant believes it to be the case.

24 Kant appears to have in mind here at least arithmetical synthesis and synthesis in metrical geometry (such as of additive quantities).

25 B757 and *Lectures on Logic,* Ac. ed., 9, sections 102, 103, 106.

26 Such as in the *Critique of Judgment,* Ac. ed., 5, sections 25-26, for synthesis in metrical geometry.

27 At least in *Prolegomena,* Ac. ed., 4, section 13. I have argued for such an interpretation elsewhere.

28 Cf. *Critique of Judgment,* Ac. ed., 5, sections 46-50. Also cf. Kant's frequent allusions to "lawfulness without laws."

29 In his *Anthropology,* Ac. ed., 7, section 39.

30 See the *Lectures on Logic,* Ac. ed., 9, section 106.

31 In his "The Ethical Significance of Kant's *Religion,*" *op. cit.,* 94.

32 J. C. Adelung, *Grammatisch-Kritisches Wörterbuch der Hochdeutschen Mundart,* vol. 4 (Breitkopf und Härtel, 1801), pp. 1547-51.

33 Daniel Sanders, *Wörterbuch der Deutschen Sprache* (Leipzig: Wiegand, 1876), p. 1059.

34 Jacob und Wilhelm Grimm, *Deutsches Wörterbuch,* vol. 14, 2, rev. L. Sütterlin (Leipzig: Hirzel, 1960), 137-65, 204-17.

35 *Nach eigenem Gefallen.*

36 *Kür* in *Willkür* is of course *choice.*

37 It similarly does not help that *voluntas* (from which *voluntary*) is free *will (freier Wille).*

38 In his *Commentary* and elsewhere.

39 In his translations collected in Kant's *Critique of Practical Reason and Other Works on the Theory of Ethics* (London, 1889).

40 In his translation of the *Critique of Judgment.* Bernard in his Glossary does translate *Willkür* as *elective will.*

41 In his translation of the *Critique of Judgment.*

42   This change from their first edition is due to Silber.

43   Francis Haywood (1838), J. M. D. Meiklejohn (1852), M. Müller (1881), and N. K. Smith (1929).

44   In his translation (with Gertrude M. Clark) of some of Kant's lectures under the title *Lectures on Philosophical Theology* (Cornell, 1978).

45   In her translation of Kant's *Anthropology* (The Hague, 1974).

46   In their translation of Kant's *Logic* (Bobbs-Merrill, 1974).

47   Section 102 of the *Logic*.

48   I draw on N. Webster, *An American Dictionary of the English Language,* rev. (Chicago: Ch. Goodrich, 1895); E. Partridge, *Origins* (London, 1958); Webster's *New Collegiate Dictionary* (Springfield, Mass., 1961).

49   I owe thanks to Chauncey Mellor and L. W. Beck for several helpful suggestions.

WERNER PLUHAR

How to Render *"Zweckmäßigkeit"* in Kant's *Third Critique*

The question of how to render this key term in Kant's *Critique of* [*the Faculty of*] *Judgment*[1] in English cannot be settled by simply appealing to either of the two standard translations, Bernard's and Meredith's.[2] One reason for this is that the two differ in how they render *Zweck, zweckmäßig,* and *zweckmäßigkeit,* Bernard using what I will call the purposiveness terminology (i.e., "purpose," "purposive," and "purposiveness"), Meredith what I will call the finality terminology (i.e., "end," "final," and "finality"). Another reason why we cannot simply appeal to either of these translations is that, as is commonly agreed and as, e.g., the *Encyclopedia of Philosophy* notes, "[b]oth versions are of poor quality," although "Meredith's is slightly the better."[3] (Indeed, how poor even Meredith's is will become apparent from a number of typical examples of mistranslations which I will have occasion to cite.) Nor can we appeal to later translators (of portions of the *Critique*), or to any of the various authors who have discussed all or part of the work, for their renderings of the term differ even more. Some of them have adopted the purposiveness terminology (e.g., Cerf and Haden, H. Cassirer, and Crawford) and others the finality terminology (e.g., Guyer and sometimes Coleman),[4] but still further terminologies appear in some of these as well as in Meredith. What all of this divergence suggests, of course, is that as yet it is not altogether settled what the correct fuller analysis of Kant's notion of *zweckmäßigkeit* will be. Moreover, it would be altogether unrealistic and

Werner Pluhar is assistant professor of philosophy, University of Pennsylvania, Uniontown.

presumptuous to try to settle that issue in a short paper such as this.[5]

What this paper does seek to do is to make possible whatever fruitful future research, by scholars not sufficiently familiar with (Kant's) German, may yet be needed to produce such a fuller analysis. What that requires is a minimal initial analysis of *Zweckmäßigkeit* sufficient to allow for the selection of a rendering for the term which will fit that minimal analysis and which therefore will avoid blocking or impeding the research for such a fuller analysis. Any rendering that fails to avoid this is obviously a mistranslation. It could fail to avoid this in a number of ways, of which I will single out and thereafter illustrate the following crucial four: Research (based on the translation — this qualification will henceforth be regarded as understood) will be blocked or impeded by any rendering of *Zweckmäßigkeit* that gives rise to (1) erasure of a distinction present in the original work, since that would block any research into that distinction, (2) implantation of a distinction not present in the original work, since that would impede research by misdirecting it toward a distinction which, as regards the work proper, is merely illusory, (3) ambiguous implantation of a distinction, or (4) ambiguous erasure of one, since either of these would impede research by creating confusion. Moreover, a mistranslation of any of these types can, of course, be aggravated further by (a) close juxtaposition of the terms responsible for the problem, (b) multiplication of the same problem, or (c) combination of it with any of the other types of mistranslation. In this paper I will be arguing in section 2 that the finality terminology is in fact a mistranslation under all four of these types. As a preparation for that argument, I will illustrate these types in section 1, using for this examples of mistranslations from Meredith other than the terminology at issue here. (I do not mean to suggest that similar examples cannot be found in Bernard.) I will then go on to argue, in section 3, that the purposiveness terminology avoids all of these problems, as well as an important further one, and, in section 4, that as regards this further problem the purposiveness terminology is also superior to all other initially plausible candidates.

1

(1) Erasure of a distinction occurs when one term is used to render two original ones, without warning (henceforth this qualification too will be regarded as understood). For example, Meredith (but similarly Bernard, Cerf, and Haden) frequently (though by no means even consistently) renders as "judgment" not only *Urteil* but also *Ur-*

teilskraft (properly "faculty of judgment," understood as a disposition).[6] Nor does the context always help to disambiguate the two. For example, in one place "for our judgment" just happens to refer to the faculty, whereas half a page earlier "upon the judgment" refers to a mere judgment; and sometimes the juxtaposition is even closer.[7] Clearly any research into what distinction Kant may or may not be intending to draw between the two is blocked by the erasure.

(2a) Implantation of a distinction occurs when two terms are used to render one original one. For example, Meredith renders the prefix *Natur-* as "natural" but also as "physical," often even in close juxtaposition.[8]   As a result, research is being misdirected toward a distinction which, as regards the work proper, is merely illusory. Note, for example, the misleading contrast in the following sentence: "Where a thing is a product of nature and yet, so regarded, has to be cognized as possible only as a physical end . . . ."[9] Similarly, the term *Naturzweck* is rendered sometimes as "natural end" but sometimes as "physical end," thus inviting misdirected research.[10]   Again, Kant's important contrast between, in the finality terminology, "natural end" and "end of nature" becomes instead a contrast between "physical end" and "end of nature."[11] (Meredith compounds this implantation by combining it with a further and independent double erasure and double implantation: For on several occasions he reverses his own renderings so that the Kantian distinction is turned fully upside down.)[12]

Note, moreover, that the implantation of the distinction between "natural" and "physical" also gives rise to the erasure of another distinction, because the term "physical" is being used to render *Natur-* but is also needed (and is in fact so used by Meredith) to render Kant's own term *physisch,* thus erasing Kant's distinction between *natürlich* and *physisch,* so that it cannot even be dismissed as unimportant, let alone become the subject of a question.[13]

(2b) But the implantation of a distinction may of course give rise to the erasure of a plainly important distinction too. Meredith, for example, renders *urteilen* as "to judge" but *beurteilen* as "to estimate" or even "to form an estimate," apparently unaware that *urteilen* and *beurteilen* mean the same, except that one is intransitive and the other transitive, whereas "to judge" can be either and thus correctly renders both. (The case is roughly similar for the corresponding nouns.) The result is again an implanted distinction that invites misdirected research, especially where the two terms are juxtaposed, as happens quite frequently.[14]   But the use of the verb and noun "estimate" in this new sense also gives rise to an important erasure: for the term is also needed to render Kant's *schätzen,* and Meredith does in fact use it that way too (sometimes he uses "estimation" rather than "estimate," but that hardly avoids the erasure).[15] The erasure thus blocks any research into the relation between Kant's *schätzen* and *beurteilen* (i.e., between "to estimate" in its proper sense and the transitive "to judge").

(3) An ambiguous implantation of a distinction occurs when an ambiguous term is used to render an unambiguous original one. Thus Meredith uses the ambiguous noun "design" to render Kant's unambiguous *Zeichnung,* which means "design" only in the sense of "pattern" but not in the sense of "intention." The distinction between the two senses of "design" is thus neither clearly implanted nor clearly not implanted, but is in fact implanted *ambiguously.* The result is, of course, confusion.

(4) An ambiguous erasure of a distinction occurs when one ambiguous term is used to render two unambiguous original ones. For example, apart from ambiguously implanting a distinction by his use of "design" to render *Zeichnung,* Meredith also produces an ambiguous erasure by using "design" again to render *Absicht* (properly "intention").[16] The distinction between the intention and the pattern, each ambiguously labeled "design," is thus neither clearly erased nor clearly not erased, but is erased ambiguously. The result is, again, confusion. Meredith again compounds the problem: he multiplies the erasure by also (at least once) using "design" for *Zweckbeziehung* (properly "reference to purpose") and "designed" for *eingerichtet* (properly "arranged"), and he combines with it a multiple implantation by rendering *Absicht* not only as "design" but also as "intention," "object in view," "attempt," and even "purpose" and (for another erasure) "end."[17]

2

Let me now apply the just-illustrated distinction of four types of mistranslation to the finality terminology. This terminology is, to be sure, initially plausible. It does indeed have a purposive sense: "end" is at least also fairly commonly used to mean *Zweck* (i.e., "purpose"), and "final" as well as "finality" are, through their link with "final cause," still readily associable with "end," even in its purposive sense. The crucial defect of the finality terminology is that it is ambiguous, indeed doubly so.

One result of this ambiguity is the ambiguous implantation of two distinctions, viz., between the purposive sense of the terminology on the one hand and each of the two other senses on the other. One of these other senses is that of "final" as meaning "decisive" (similarly for "finality"). It is suggested (ambiguously) in such occurrences as the following: "the . . . finality in the essence of things," "the . . . final specification of nature," "the final action," "for which the form . . . is final," "the greatest finality in the construction of this form," "finality for our cognitive faculty," or "such . . . adjustments of nature as are considered final."[18] Then there is the temporal sense of this terminology, suggested (ambiguously) in occurrences like these: "its final nexus," "the final form," "the final harmony," "their . . . final effects," "these final products," "final adaptations," "the finality of the things of nature in general," "its final production," "estimated as final," or "nothing . . . but what is final when . . .";[19] and similarly: "the end of his existence," "the end of the real existence of a natural being," "the end of the real existence of nature itself," "this cause look[s] to an end," "In such a product nothing is . . . without an end," and "the ultimate end."[20] That this twofold implantation gives rise to confusion it would be difficult to deny.

Moreover, Kant himself uses the word *Ende,* mainly in its standard sense, i.e., the temporal one, so that Meredith now finds himself forced to use the ambiguous rendering "end" not only purposively but temporally too. The result of that is an ambiguous erasure. (Even Kant's own rare purposive use of *Ende*—probably already becoming archaic in his time, except in such compounds as *Endursache* and *Endzweck*—needs to be distinguished from *Zweck* if the distinction is to be capable of so much as dismissal; but Meredith renders that *Ende* as "ulterior end."[21]) Kant's temporal *Ende* is found sometimes by itself, but most often in compounds. As an example of the former, Kant's *ohne Ende* (i.e., "without end") is rendered by Meredith as "endless," but *zwecklos* (i.e., "purposeless") comes out similarly as "without end," the important distinction between the two having been erased.[22] But the problem is most severe where these two senses of the finality terminology occur in one and the same compound word, viz., in Kant's very important term *Endzweck* (i.e., "[temporally] final purpose"). Although Meredith refrains from rendering it as "end-end," he finds himself forced to do the next worst thing: he renders it as "final end." This extremely close juxtaposition of the temporal and the purposive sense of this terminology results in a severely ambiguous erasure. Thus, on occasion "final end" sounds wholly temporal, as e.g., in "the final end of the existence of a world . . ." or in "the ultimate and final end of the presence here of the world";[23] but more often it is the purposive sense of "final" which interferes, especially in the several

places where "final end" is densely juxtaposed with the finality terminology in its purposive sense; thus, e.g., "final end" is found just
before "final action" or just after "final nexus" (the latter two with "final" in the purposive sense), and so on in many more cases.[24] The
resultant ambiguous erasure gives rise to considerable confusion.

On a number of occasions, Meredith's cumulative awareness of
this problem and its origin in the finality terminology seems to have
prompted him to abandon it temporarily, rendering *zweckmäßig* instead suddenly (and again without warning) as "adapted to ends,"
"suitable," "teleological," "wise,"[25] or even as "purposively adapted"
or outright as "purposive,"[26] thus eliminating some confusion but at
the cost of implanting numerous further distinctions that misdirect
any research into this key notion. These implantations, moreover,
are in turn combined with further, but independent, erasures. For
the term "purpose" is also quite frequently used to render certain
prepositions (such as *um* and *zu*), and *wozu* even becomes "What is
the end and purpose."[27] Again, even *Material* (properly "material") is
once rendered as "purpose"; so is *Behuf* (properly "sake"); and so is
Absicht (properly "intention"), so that together with *zuträglich* ("condu-
cive" or "profitable") we actually get the expression "to adapt . . . to . . .
purposes," which Meredith fails to set off against the expression
"adapted to ends," which he sometimes uses to render *zweckmäßig*.[28]
None of this purpose and even purposiveness terminology appears in
Meredith's index, however, except for one occurrence of "purpose"
in one subheading under "finality,"[29] and in that case the word which
actually appears on the indexed pages is in fact not "purpose," but
"end."

It would be difficult to exaggerate the degree to which all of these
implantations and erasures, ambiguous and unambiguous, combine
to impede or outright block any research into the notion of *Zweckmäßigkeit* by means of that translation. Most importantly, all of them
except for the last-mentioned few are occasioned by the finality terminology itself. Let us therefore look at the alternative candidates, beginning with the purposiveness terminology.

3

Clearly *Zweck* is rendered at least as well by "purpose" as it is by "end,"
in ordinary language as well as in philosophy. (I am disregarding
its etymology, which happens to be unhelpful.)[30] Moreover, the
purposiveness terminology does not share the disastrous ambiguity

of the finality terminology.   The question which remains for this
paper, therefore, in the absence of a fuller analysis of *Zweckmäßigkeit*
which our rendering is supposed to make possible, is this: what minimal part of such an analysis must a rendering satisfy if it is to avoid
impeding future research into the notion?

Obviously, whatever the exact force of *-mäßig* may be in this case
(perhaps "like," or — somewhat more literally — "com-mensur-ate
with"), an adequate rendering of Kant's notion must not conflict
with Kant's own explicit characterizations of it.   In particular, it
must not conflict with any of the at least twenty-six adjectives which
Kant uses to distinguish types of "purposiveness" (as I will henceforth
for the simplicity call it, by way of anticipation of my conclusion).[31]
The adjective "material," e.g., is intended to imply a "matter," i.e., a
purpose.[32] The term "purposiveness" must therefore not rule out the
presence of a purpose, putative or actual.   Moreover, even mere
geometric figures are said by Kant to be purposive in the sense of
being "suitable" (i.e., objectively purposive) for "all sorts of purposes"
in mathematics.[33]   Thus the question becomes: should the term
"purposiveness" perhaps imply (at least a putative) purpose, or should
it be noncommittal in that regard?   On either alternative, does the
term satisfy the condition?

The answer hinges on Kant's notion of aesthetic purposiveness,
which is what "aesthetic judgments of reflection" are said to be about.
For this is the famous "purposiveness *without* a purpose," without not
only an actual purpose but even the representation of one.[34]   It is
said to be formal as well as aesthetic and, as such, subjective (rather
than intellectual and objective).[35]   It lacks a concept with which to
refer to an objective purpose, but it also lacks any reference to a subjective purpose (such as the sensation of agreeableness).[36]   It thus
lacks any purpose (or "interest"), objective or subjective,[37] but is
"without a purpose," "disinterested," and in that sense "free."[38]   So
far this notion of a "purposiveness without a purpose" seems un-
problematic.   Indeed, as Guyer points out, it is not new with Kant
(although Guyer's citation from Aristotle is unconvincing).[39]

H. Cassirer agrees that "Kant's general idea is quite clear" and he
even quotes Kant's statement that this aesthetic purposiveness is independent of any purpose (or concept of one), "subjective or objective." But then, as if he felt after all that purposiveness requires a
purpose, he asks, "In what sense then can we speak of purposiveness
at all?"[40] Cassirer's "solution" is that there is after all a purpose, but
merely a subjective rather than an objective one, merely a purpose

"in relation to the mind,"[41] viz., the production of a harmony of the knowledge faculties in free play for the sake of knowledge in general.[42] Cassirer repeats the same slip from "without a purpose" to "with a subjective purpose" in the context of art (as distinct from taste).[43] (In the context of the sublime, as distinct from the beautiful, he similarly slips from "subjectively purposive" to "not at all purposive.")[44] But clearly this is not a solution at all, since it merely contradicts Kant's explicit insistence that there is no purpose here, subjective or objective. Or does Kant share this inconsistency?

Although such expressions as "purposive for" and other features of Kant's account may suggest a purpose,[45] Kant in fact takes pains to avoid that implication: what is implied in aesthetic purposiveness is not a purpose but merely something analogous,[46] something purposelike (*zweckähnlich*).[47]   Guyer calls aesthetic purposiveness the "aesthetic analogue of systematicity"[48] and refers to it always (except for one slip)[49] as an "objective," i.e., an indeterminate (preconceptual) analogue of a purpose.

Moreover, Kant also characterizes purposiveness as a lawlikeness (*Gesetzmäßigkeit*).[50]   That original term is in fact, at least in most instances, correctly rendered as "lawlikeness" (compounds of "law" or lex similar in structure to "purposive" are already taken) is clear in part from Kant's characterization of "purposiveness without a purpose" as again a "free" lawlikeness and indeed as a "lawlikeness" without a law;[51] Meredith's rendering of this as a "conformity to law without a law" sounds outright contradictory. Guyer, who follows Meredith for the most part, replaces Meredith's rendering here by the still at least perplexing "lawfulness without a law."[52] Indeed, it is presumably so as to avoid just such a contradiction or perplexity that no one shows any inclination to render *Zweckmäßigkeit* itself as "conformity to purpose," and only one (Coleman) occasionally as "purposefulness."[53] (Crawford's equation of purposiveness with rulegovernedness, let alone with designedness, is questionable for the same reason.)[54] Indeed, Meredith seems to sense the misplaced implication of a law in "conformity to law" when he replaces the expression (again without warning) simply with "order" and "conformable to law" with "uniform" and with "authoritative" (thus implanting several more distinctions). [55] Similarly, he correctly renders *regelmäßig* as "regular" rather than as "conformable to rule."[56] On the other hand, one does wonder whether Kant's own occasional switch from *gesetzmäßig* to *gesetzlich* is meant to be merely terminological,[57] or rather to indicate (at least on some occasions) that he now wishes to be less noncommittal about the implication of a law, as the latter term suggests (in which case "lawgovernedness" might be an adequate rendering).[58] That question, however, is blocked by Meredith, since he renders both these expressions as "conformity to law" and thus erases any distinction into which to inquire. This much is clear, however: that Kant's addition of "without a law" to whatever other term, so as to have the combined expression characterize his "purposiveness without a purpose," does underline that any adequate rendering of *Zweckmäßigkeit* must avoid not only ruling out a purpose, putative or actual, but must also avoid implying one, at least in one of its senses.

Consider now some of the remaining initially plausible candidates. "Purposelike" is already taken, viz., to render *zweckähnlich.* So of course is Meredith's (one-time) "teleological," for Kant's extremely frequent and quite independently important *teleologisch* (which moreover has a different meaning from *zweckmäßig* anyway). Coleman's "purposeful" must be dismissed as not being sufficiently noncommittal, as must be on the same ground Meredith's occasional "adapted to ends" as well as Cassirer's sporadic and rather wild "pre-adapted" (which he contrasts with "ill-adapted" for *zweckwidrig,* even though that term too needs to be noncommittal and is best rendered as "contrapurposive" or "counter-purposive," in contrast both to "purposive" and to "nonpurposive" [for *unzweckmäßig*]).[59] The same applies to Meredith's occasional "suitable" (which moreover best renders Kant's *tauglich,* which he uses to characterize objective purposiveness only),[60] as well as to "fitting" (which moreover best renders Kant's *schicklich*) and to any synonym thereof, and even to "functional" (which moreover has other wrong connotations in addition).

The term "purposive" on the other hand (similarly for the noun) actually fits rather well. The ending "-ive" does suggest "-like" and thus makes the term basically noncommittal. And that is indeed how it appears, e.g., in Webster; its basic sense is there given as "serving or effecting a useful function though not necessarily as a result of deliberate design"; moreover, that the commitment being avoided concerns not merely "deliberate design" but any purpose, deliberate or not, is clear from the single example given for elucidation: "a work of art may be without a purpose, yet purposive."[61] The second sense given for the term differs with regard to that very commitment and is thus appropriately equated with "purposeful." (A third sense is restructed to "purposivism" in psychology and may be disregarded here.) Does the ambiguity between the basic sense and the one derivative one implant a distinction? It does not, provided that *zweckmäßig* is ambiguous in the same way. That may indeed turn out to be the case.[62] On the other hand, the very fact that we have a choice between singling out the noncommittal sense alone and making use of both senses, does give us a welcome openness. If future research on *Zweckmäßigkeit* shows it to be unambiguous and thus purely noncommittal, then we need merely drop the committal second sense of "purposiveness" as an alternative and insert an appropriate warning to that effect in a translation of the *Critique*. In the meantime, no research will have been blocked or impeded.

I conclude that the purposiveness terminology is crucially superior to all other initially plausible candidates, and especially to the finality terminology.

NOTES

1   I am indebted to Professor Lewis White Beck for helpful information.

2   Citations from the original refer to *Kants Werke, Akademie Textausgabe* (henceforth abbreviated "AT") (Berlin: Walter de Gruyter, 1968), which photomechanically reproduces unchanged the text of *Kants gesammelte Schriften*, Königlich Preußische Akademie der Wissenschaften (Berlin, 1908), v. 5 (same volume in AT). Citations from the "First Introduction" are from the same 1908 original, v. 20 (henceforth abbreviated as "F"). The translations of the *Critique* by Bernard and Meredith carry the title (*The* [Meredith]) *Critique of Judgement;* one is by J. H. Bernard (New York: Hafner, 1974 (1951, originally 1892)), the other by James Creed Meredith (London: Oxford University Press, 1973 (1952)), the latter being a reprint from two separate 1928 editions of the two component works. References to Meredith will be prefixed "M" followed by "I" or "II" for the respective component works (which have separate pagination in Meredith).

3   (1967), v. 4, p. 323c.

4   Immanuel Kant, *Analytic of the Beautiful,* trans. Walter Cerf (Indianapolis: Bobbs-Merrill, 1963). Immanuel Kant, *First Introduction to the Critique of Judgment,* trans. James Haden (Indianapolis: Bobbs-Merrill, 1965). H. W. Cassirer, *A Commentary on Kant's Critique of Judgment* (London: Methuen, 1938). Donald W. Crawford, *Kant's Aesthetic Theory* (Madison: University of Wisconsin Press, 1974). Paul Guyer, *Kant and the Claims of Taste* (Cambridge: Harvard University Press, 1979). Francis X. J. Coleman, *The Harmony of Reason: A Study in Kant's Aesthetics* (Pittsburgh: University of Pittsburgh Press, 1974). Citations from these authors will give simply the author's name followed by page, paragraph and line, a minus sign indicating that the count is from the bottom, a plus sign not followed by a number meaning "ff."

5   For an excellent in-depth study (written in German), see Konrad Marc-Wogau, "Vier Studien zu Kants Kritik der Urteilskraft," *Uppsala Universitets Årsskrift* (Appelbergs Boktryckeriaktiebolag), no. 2 (1938); second study: "Wesen und Arten der Zweckmässigkeit," pp. 44-213.

6   E.g., MI 4.31 = AT 168.24 and MI 6.11 = AT 169.29, but contrast MI 5.12 + 26 = AT 169.1 + 13.

7   E.g., MI 100.16 = AT 252.30 vs. MI 99.33 = AT 252.16; MI 100.17/20 = AT 252.32/33.

8   E.g., MII 18.4 + 8 = AT 370.33 + 34, MII 23.24 + 25 = AT 375.10 + 12.

9   MII 19.29/30 = AT 372.15, and cf. MII 21.5/8 = AT 373.14/16.

10   E.g., MI 34.24 + 35.11 = AT 193.14 + 33, and cf. *Naturding* being rendered as "natural thing" but shortly thereafter as "physical thing": MII 14.33 + 15.12 = AT 368.18 + 30.

11   MII 27.14 + 15 = AT 378.12 + 13.

12   MII 15.5 + 14 vs. 18 + 20 = AT 368.23 + 30 vs. 35, MII 30.3 = AT 380.19, MII 14.9 vs. 15.20 = AT 367.32 vs. 368.35.

13   E.g., MII 28.4 = AT 378.31 and MII 29.16 = AT 379.35, MII 152.32 = AT 477.7, and cf. MII 32.25 + = AT 382.20 + .

14   E.g., MI 101.6/12 = AT 253.16/22. Kant's (?) equation (F 211.17/18) of *beurteilen* (*diiudicare*) with reflective *urteilen* is neither mentioned nor adhered to elsewhere (see e.g., AT 190.13/18, 213.2/12, 218.32/36, 245.19/24, 281.5/6, 365.11/22).   Kant realized no doubt that the built-in transitivity/intransitivity distinction was both inescapable and needed.   Moreover, in the first *Critique* (A 132/B 171) he had characterized any *urteilen* as a distinguishing [i.e., *diiudicare*].

15   MI 78.6/7 = AT 234.11, and cf. MI 98.10 + = AT 251.1 +, MI 101.12/15 = AT 253.21/24; but cf. Guyer's use of "estimation" as a synonym for "judgment": Guyer, 113.3.5. On at least two occasions, moreover, Meredith renders *Beurteilung* as "critical judgment" (MII 80.25 = AT 420.23 and MII 159 n.-4 = AT 482.33), whereas elsewhere *Beurteilung* becomes simply "critical" (MII 101.24 = AT 437.13/14) or for that matter even "reflection" (MII 109.25 = AT 443.16/17)! On the other hand, *Urteil* is sometimes rendered as "verdict" rather than as "judgment": e.g., MII 109.24 = AT 443.14.

16   E.g., MI 67.23 = AT 225.17 vs. MII 33.21 = AT 383.10.

17   MII 117n.8 = AT 449.26/27; MII 9.9 = AT 363.34; MI 167.11/12 = AT 306.27; MII 145n.14 = AT 471.19; MII 148.32 = AT 474.9; MII 30.15 = AT 380.25; MII 106.15 = AT 440.33; MII 96.3 = AT 432.28 + MII 163.5 = AT 484.36. On at least one occasion *absichtlich* is even rendered as "far-seeing" (MII 96.22 = AT 433.7)!

18   MII 11.15 = AT 365.24/25; MI 28.18/19 = AT 188.8/9; MII 101.13/14 = AT 437.5; MI 32.31/32 = AT 191.33/34, MI 77.18 = AT 233.27/28, MI 23.25 (emphasis removed) = AT 184.8/9 and MI 28.23 = AT 188.12/13 (the plural is

not in the original) and cf. MI 100.16 = AT 252.30, MI 28.6 = AT 187.35; MII 34.20/21 = AT 384.7/8. By the same token, Meredith at least once renders *Endabsicht* (properly "[temporally] final intention") as "real end" (MII 96.3 = AT 432.28)!

19   MII 59.21 = AT 404.19, MI 71.16/17 = AT 228.26 and MII 52.14 = AT 399.3, MI 32.19 = AT 191.22, MII 26.23/24 = AT 377.30, MII 32.12 = AT 382.8/9 and cf. MII 123.29/30 = AT 454.22 and MII 136n.-4 = AT 464.33, MII 108.14 = AT 442.17, MII 32.33 = AT 382.27/28, MII 44.13/14 = AT 393.1, MII 27.12 = AT 378.10/11, MII 28.20 = AT 379.8/9.

20   MII 100n.-2/-1 = AT 436.36/37, MII 87.34 = AT 426.10, MII 27.20 = AT 378.18, MII 14.24 = AT 368.10/11, MII 88.9 + = AT 426.18 + (emphasis removed).

21   MII 87.11 = AT 425.26.

22   MII 25.1 = AT 376.14, MI 104.8 = AT 255.33, and cf. MII 117.12 = AT 449.9. Elsewhere still Meredith renders *zwecklos* as "meaningless" (MII 85.3 = AT 423.35) and as "senseless" (MII 138n.-1 = AT 465.36).

23   MII 98.0 = AT 434.5 (emphasis removed), MII 153.11/12 = AT 477.15/16. Cf. also MII 108.18/19 = AT 442.21, MII 108.25 = AT 442.26, MII 108.27 = AT 442.28.

24   MII 101.8/14 = AT 437.1/5, MII 14.13/15 = AT 367.37/368.1; MI 38.1/13 = AT 196.1/10, MII 27.12/17 = AT 378.10/15, MII 86.13/89.28 = AT 425.4/427.26, MII 98.0/23 = AT 434.5/435.4.

25   E.g., MII 88.4 = AT 426.13, MII 89.14/15 = AT 427.16, MII 86.18 = AT 425.8; MII 79.21 = AT 419.23; MII 81.1 = AT 420.28; MII 90.6 = AT 428.1. Cf. *Zweck* as "goal": MII 147.24 = AT 473.9.

26   MII 96.33 = AT 433.17/18, MII 74.5 = AT 415.15, MII 80.9 = AT 420.9, MII 88.32 = AT 427.2, MII 97.4 = AT 433.20, and cf. MII 9.6 = AT 363.30 just before "final" as well as "purposive" in the sense of *absichtlich* (whereas elsewhere "purposeless" is used to render *zwecklos*: MII 80.18 = AT 420.16).

27   MII 86.13/91.1 = AT 425.4/427.32, MII 88.27 = AT 426.34. But elsewhere *wozu* is rendered as "for what end": MII 98.4 = AT 434.11, MII 98.13 = AT 434.19, MII 99.25 = AT 435.27, MII 100 n.-13 = AT 436.28.

28   MII 13.6 = AT 367.5, MII 157.15 = AT 480.22, MII 14.32 = AT 368.18/22, MII 106.25 + 109.5 = AT 440.33 + 442.35, MII 159.22/23 = AT 482.12. Cf. also "end" for *absicht:* MII 96.3 + 163.5 = AT 432.28 + 484.36!

29   MI 234, the reference to pages 62 and 69.

30   *Zweck* originally referred to the nail (cf. *Heftzwecke, Reißzwecke,* as well as the presumably cognate English "tack") which was used by marksmen to fasten a target [German *Zielscheibe*—one may be tempted to suspect a similar relationship between *Ziel* ["goal," "aim"] and τέλος] at its center and thus came itself to be an aim or "goal": cf. *Handbuch philosophischer Grundbegriffe,* eds. Hermann Krings, Hans Michael Baumgartner, and Christoph Wild (Munich: Kösel-Verlag, 1973-74), v. 3, *Zweck,* p. 1817; also *Der Sprach-Brockhaus,* ed. F. A. Brockhaus (Wiesbaden: Eberhard Brockhaus, 1951), *zwecks,* 797c.

31 E.G., "aesthetic" AT 270.33 + 362.11, "logical" F216.20 and cf. AT 192.14, "intellectual" AT 362.10/11, "ideal" [*idealisch*] AT 188.12, "formal" AT 181.13 + 361.6, "figurative" F 233.36/234.1, "material" AT 362.5, "subjective" AT 190.1 + 359.3/4, "objective" AT 193.15 + 359.2, "real" AT 193.14 + 364.5, "empirical" AT 364.23/24, "relative" AT 366.25, "absolute" F 217.24 and cf. AT 369.2, "external" AT 368.32, "internal" AT 366.26, "intentional" AT 253.35 + 383.8, "unintentional" AT 391.19, spontaneous [*spontanea*] F 235.8, "natural" F 235.8 and cf. 390.37, "technical" AT 382.18, "practical" AT 181.9, "teleological" F 233.23 and cf. AT 270.4, "organic" F 234.9/11, "plastic" F 234.6/11, "accidental" AT 368.12 and cf. AT 186.27/30, "transcendental" AT 185.17/18. For a similar list and an attempt to systematize it, see Giorgio Tonelli, "Von den verschiedenen Bedeutungen des Wortes Zweckmäßigkeit in der Kritik der Urteilskraft," *Kant-Studien,* 49, 2 (1957-58).

32 AT 220.28/29, and cf. "thing" (AT 192.22) and "real" (AT 193.14 + 364.5).

33 AT 366.9/10 + 362.8 (emphasis added).

34 E.g., AT 220.22/23 + 221.22/23 + 241.15 (emphasis added); AT 220.17/19.

35 E.g., AT 190.2, AT 362.10.

36 AT 205.25/206.25, AT 216.30/217.4.

37 AT 221.7/9 + 221.23.

38 AT 204.21 + 240.21/24.

39 Guyer, 55.-1.-3/-1. The quote is from Aristotle's *Physics,* b. ii, ch. 8 [199b26 +]. Aristotle is actually talking about deliberateness, and an observed one at that. Cf. *Aristotle's Physics,* trans. Hippocrates G. Apostle (Bloomington: Indiana University Press, 1969), p. 40.1.1/2.

40 Cassirer, 172.3.5 + -2, 271.2.-2, 204.2-6/-5, 204.-1.1 +, 205.2.1 +.

41 Cassirer, 205.3.-1/4.1, 205.3.7/8; 146.-1.-2 +.

42 Cassirer, 222.1.9 and cf. AT 189.32/190.2.

43 Cassirer, 206.1.6/-4 + 277.3.12/-1.

44 Cassirer, 229.2.4/8 and cf. 237.4.3/7. Even Marc-Wogau speaks of an indeterminate purpose: "Vier Studien . . . ," 84.1.3.

45 AT 184.9 + 188.12/13, F 233.21/22; F 233.35; AT 190.10 + 252.30, F 221.5 + 232.36; and cf. AT 187.35.

46 AT 181.10; cf. "as if": AT 181.1.

47 AT 390.34/35.

48 Guyer, 51.1.5/6.

49 See "end" in an expression quoted from Kant (AT 242.18/19) but which actually goes with determination and so is misplaced here: Guyer, 84.-1.3.

50 F 217.28, and cf. F 243.5/6.

51 AT 241.11/16 (emphasis added).

52 MI 86.22 (emphasis added); Guyer, 91.-1.-4 (emphasis added).

53 Coleman, 51.2.-2 and 52.2.-3.

54 Crawford, 68.2.5/6.

55 MII 4.2 = AT 359.23, MII 115.34 = AT 448.12, MII 48.11 = AT 395.35.

56 MII 9.29 = AT 364.18.

57 Consider e.g. the similarity in two formulations which differ with respect to that term: AT 404.27/28 vs. F 217.28 (and AT 241.14/16).

58 MII 59.30 + 33 = AT 404.27/28. Cf. also *"pflichtmäßig"* ("duty-conforming"): AT 469.1.

59 Coleman, see n. 53, above; MII 88.4 + 89.14/15 = AT 426.13 + 427.16; Cassirer, 222.1.-5, and cf. AT 245.21 + and 252.30.

60 AT 362.7/8.

61 *Webster's Third New International Dictionary of the English Language* (1966).

62 Cf. Marc-Wogau, "Vier Studien . . . ," 44.1.13/17.

HANS H. RUDNICK

Translation and Kant's
Anschauung, Verstand, and *Vernunft*

Translation means the "carrying over" of meaning from a source language into a target language with the intention of performing this task with as much accuracy as possible. In this particular instance we know that the German and English languages are rather close relatives within the Indo-European language family. So it may appear that translation from the one language into the other should not cause major problems as far as questions of semantic equivalence and cultural translatability are concerned. In addition, translation into English might seem an easy task since the English language has, without doubt, one of the largest vocabularies of all languages because two languages, the language of the Normans and the language of the Anglo-Saxons, grew together during the centuries after the Norman Conquest. There should be a wealth of terminology available in order to obtain linguistic equivalence which would allow an uncomplicated and clear transfer of meaning from German into English.

However, in spite of dealing with closely related Indo-European languages, and in spite of the abundance of available vocabulary in English, the "carrying over" of Kant's philosophical terminology and meaning into proper English creates major difficulties. In the following paragraphs I shall address myself first to the general theoretical problems and second to the particular and practical problems facing the Kant translator.

Hans H. Rudnick is associate professor of English, Southern Illinois University, Carbondale.

1

The question of linguistic equivalence arises as soon as the translating of Kant is contemplated. Besides the basic syntactical differences between both languages, i.e., English is governed by a strict analytic syntax whereas German uses a more flexible synthetic syntax, Kant complicates the German sentence structure frequently beyond tolerance because of endlessly long sentences that sometimes even lack grammatical clarity and completeness. Such formal complexity of expression in sentence structure causes, naturally, also confusion on the semantic level. Consequently, reading Kant with understanding is by itself a trying task on the syntactic as well as semantic levels. Kant's German is as challenging to the native German reader as Jaspers', Heidegger's, or Jean Paul's German; it is even more demanding because of the virtual linguistic untranslatability of certain terms which are used by Kant in a sense that runs contrary to the received language-bound meaning of common usage. For example, Kant, "the smasher of everything" (Moses Mendelssohn), the ardent admirer of Rousseau's style, told himself that "I must read Rousseau until the beauty of his expression does no longer disturb me, and I can then obtain a rational over-all view."[1] As a result of such critical detachment and rationality, necessarily and absolutely inconsiderate of tradition, Kant used key concepts of his own thought, like idealism, and transcendentalism, subject and object with just about the opposite meaning of their conventional philosophical use. As a result the general reader finds himself confused as much as the philosophical reader since both are encountering an unfamiliar usage of terms which in themselves are terms of regular usage but, as it turns out, cannot be taken at face value. Instead, these terms must be redefined from within the Kantian context of thought and attributed a new semantic context which applies solely to Kant and neither to the previously established general usage nor, for example, to the philosophical *intuitio*-tradition based on Plato, Aristotle, Augustine, Descartes, Leibniz, and Locke.

The translator finds himself entangled in this complicated net of language, semantics, philosophy, and culture. It is the most challenging, agonizing, and intellectually rewarding experience for a bilingual and bi-cultural person. The labors lying ahead will be tedious, trying, and financially unrewarding because it is still a widely-held opinion that "the art of translation is a subsidiary art and derivative. On this account it has never been granted the dignity of original work, and has suffered too much in the general judgment of letters."[2]

And yet, there will be translators, especially among the academics, who take on this labor of love in order to perform the nearly impossible task of "carrying" the achievements of one culture's personalities "over" into another culture. The task is formidable particularly in the case of Immanuel Kant whose difficult style and semantic complications have already been characterized above. Kant is a prime example for the veracity of Edward Sapir's statement about each language's separate structure and the separate semantic and social reality resulting necessarily from it. Sapir states:

> No two languages are ever sufficiently similar to be considered as represent-
> ing the same social reality. The worlds in which different societies live are
> distinct worlds, not merely the same world with different labels attached.[3]

Kant as the "the smasher of everything" (*der Alleszermalmer*) certainly not only lived in a different society with its distinct world but, because of his genius, created a different world himself within which he felt strong enough to change the labels by altering their semantic contents. Kant in this context is, for the translator, like a poet whose changing of labels and perspectives cannot be questioned but must be accepted. It is, therefore, further discouragement to the translator if he heeds Roman Jakobson's statement that poetic art is technically untranslatable and can at best only be creatively transposed. The expectation of achieving full equivalency of meaning must be given up if the translator faces his task realistically. There can be no full equivalence through translation. Significations only function naturally within a given culture. Dealing with Kant complicates cultural signification further since he marks a fresh beginning, a new perspective, a Copernican Revolution in philosophical and cultural signification. The competent translator must recognize this fact as, long ago, it had been recognized by King Alfred (reigned 871-899) who translated the *Cura Pastoralis* into English *hwilum word be worde, hwilum andgiet of andgiete* (sometimes word by word, sometimes sense by sense) or in the words of Roman translators who followed the Horacian and Ciceronian tradition *non verbum de verbo, sed sensum exprimere de sensu* (not translating word for word, but sense for sense).

The translator must be aware of how significations function within a given culture. He works with criteria that transcend the purely linguistic realm; he has to engage in a process of decoding and recoding for which there do not yet exist any rules of operation. Such interlingual transposition involves semiotic and cultural transformations which must be performed by the translator on the basis of his own semiotic and cultural knowledge and experience. For the Kant translator there is no way of escaping into anonymity. He knows, on the one hand, that the exact word-for-word transfer of meaning is impossible and he also knows, on the other hand, that the telescoping or omitting of difficult expressions is an immoral act that does not serve the established purpose. The emphasis of a translation must focus on an authentic transfer of meaning for the reader in the other culture. It will probably be impossible to transfer or even impose the value system of the source language's culture onto the target language culture, but, it appears, the translator should not refrain from transmitting as much of the source language's culture as educated judgment allows. Such transmitting of another culture's value system must assume an open-minded reader who can be expected to enjoy intellectual curiosity, independent thinking, and a dislike of linguistic and semantic clichés.

Kant is a case in point where a reader must employ all his ability of perception so that he can reach the necessary freedom from previous concepts in order to be open enough for Kant's demanding thought processes. Kant's thinking alone, however, is not the primary difficulty. Had he used a style and manner of argumentation with which a reader would feel comfortable, Kant would be half as hard to understand. In addition to the new semantic contents of certain key concepts, Kant has formulated his thoughts in extremely complicated grammatical structures which arouse even in native German speakers the reaction of a linguistic *tour de force*. Since the English language is characterized by virtue of its analytic syntax as a language of short sentences following clear grammatical patterns, a successful English translation of Kant's writings would definitely be preferable to reading the original in German. The reader of the English translation would only have to struggle with Kant's thinking process and not also with his complicated style. The successful English translation would, ideally, represent the invariant content of the philosophical work within the dynamic relationship rendered between the source language and the target language by the individual translator. Syntactic, semantic, and pragmatic components of the translation process, however, create only a quasi-equivalence between the two languages and their individual cultural settings. The text of the source language is in itself explicit, limited, and structured because of its organization as a meaningful text. Identity with that original text cannot be obtained in the target language. The best that can be reached on these grounds is a quasi-identity which differs from translator to translator as to linguistic accidentals but not as to the semantic essentials of the text.

It is a fact that linguistic and cultural untranslatability exists. In these cases, which an experienced translator can sense, the reader should be provided with a concept or term grounded in his own cultural context. If this is achieved, the reader of the target language is given the opportunity of particularizing the expressed thoughts according to his cultural view. The basic typological features of the original text are thereby "carried over" into the target language without causing difficulty to the reader's understanding. The full linguistic structure of the original, however, can hardly find adequate expression in a translation.

Translation has become an enterprise that nowadays is concerned with the creation of a vernacular text in the same manner as Dante, Wycliffe, Tyndale, and Luther were engaged in creating vernacular texts. Since the command of foreign languages is no longer widespread even among the higher educated, the translation of important texts has become increasingly necessary. As it has been the case with Bible translations, successive translations have also been prepared of Kant's works. Pioneering translations are generally not as successful as later revisions based upon them. The later translator does not have to struggle so hard with the entire complexity of the linguistic and semantic transfer process, instead he can use a pre-existent base and improve on it by being more concerned with finding the most adequate expression available in the target language. Furthermore, later translators have less difficulty with the approximation of cultural equivalency. Comparing, for example, the quality of several translations of Kant's *Critique of Pure Reason,* it is striking by how far Kemp Smith's translation is superior to Meiklejohn's.

This should not be surprising since Kemp Smith's translation (begun 1913, published 1929) appeared seventy-four years after Meiklejohn's (1855) and forty-eight years after Max Müller's (1881). Kemp Smith acknowledges his advantages by saying "I have greatly profited by the work of my two predecessors."[4] Kemp Smith praises Meiklejohn's "happy gift . . . of making Kant speak in language that reasonably approximates to English idiom," whereas Max Müller's merit is described as giving "greater accuracy in rendering passages in which a specially exact appreciation of the niceties of German idiom happens to be important for the sense."[5] The philosophical shortcomings of both prior translators are characterized by Kemp Smith as having "labored . . . under the disadvantage of not having made any very thorough study of the Critical Philosophy,"[6] which pretty much delivers the decisive *coup de grâce* to the usefulness of a translation on the semantic level.

Kemp Smith's remarks about the achievement of his predecessors also reflect the prevailing status of translation studies[7] at the time when these translations were published. Victorian translators declared that a translator should retain the peculiarities of the source language wherever possible. "Quaint archaic English . . . with just the right outlandish flavor" would successfully "disguise" the inequity of the original, G. A. Simcox argued in a review of William Morris' translation of *The Story of the Volsungs and Nibeluungs*.[8] Carlyle used Germanisms in his translations from the German without considering the English reader's difficulty with such nonidiomatic language. Respect for the original and its language was so strong that Victorian translators addressed themselves to the cultivated reader with whom they offered to share the enriching experience of encountering the original text together. Since the cultivated reader represented only a fraction of the reading public, translations carried a nationalistic flavor and did not cater to the ideal of universal literacy and culture. Translation was geared toward a minority, toward scholars. Matthew Arnold stated that the translator should "not trust to what the ordinary English reader thinks of him; he will be taking the blind for his guide."[9] Another example for the exclusive nature of Victorian translators is Henry Wadsworth Longfellow's remark: "The business of a translator is to report what the author says, not to explain what he means."[10] Translations following such a dictum will necessarily be literal, pedantic, and of extremely limited use to the majority of readers.

It is obvious that more consideration must be given to the modern reader who is no longer in a position of commanding several foreign languages. For the modern reader translations must be the result of a careful and meticulous linguistic and semantic "carrying over" of meaning into his vernacular. There is no other successful communication possible involving a text in a source language and a text rendered into a target language through translation. Readers at the times of Meiklejohn and Max Müller still knew foreign languages in greater numbers than today. Many of them might have been able to read the original and the translation simultaneously, thereby, while testing their own linguistic and semantic learning, avoiding most of the pitfalls of a faulty translation. Today, however, when readers are nearly exclusively monolingual, reliable translations like the one by Kemp Smith are absolutely necessary.

Another complication arises when Kant is being considered for translation into English. This problem is related to the fundamentally different cultural traditions which have evolved in both nations. Different developments on the linguistic and semantic levels of both languages make the achieving of quasi-equivalence even harder or nearly impossible. Kant's thinking is already by itself rather foreign to the Anglo-American frame of mind. The translator is, therefore, faced with the fact that he is dealing with a relatively alien subject which is hard to understand because of its culturally unfamiliar concepts and unorthodox semantic significations.

2

Few translators of Kant's works have addressed the problem of proper transfer of meaning from one language into another. Victorian translators saw no need of drawing attention to the cultural, linguistic, and semantic differences between the languages of nations because, for these translators, such differences were understood as being part and parcel of the encounter with another nation's intellectual and cultural products. Translators did not have to make concessions to the readers of their work because readers were expected to deal with the particular text on its own terms. Victorian readers, who, of course, had a better command of the major foreign languages than modern readers, were to meet the translated text head-on and learn by being directly confronted with the linguistic and semantic strangeness of a text in their own language, of the difference and foreignness of the society which originally produced the text.[11] It is, therefore, not surprising, but rather typical, that translators like Meiklejohn, Max Müller, and even Kemp Smith, who belongs to a later epoch, do not address this question.

Among the Kantian notions whose semantic implications as philosophical concepts are hardest to translate into proper English are *Anschauung, Verstand,* and *Vernunft,* which are generally rendered in the English language as "intuition," "understanding," and "reason."[12]

It is obvious that these three terms incorporate the epistemological paradigm of our modern scientific age; they represent its ontology to a considerable degree. It could be expected that terms so deeply integrated into Western intellectual history should easily find semantic equivalents in such closely related languages of the same language family as English and German. But this is not so. The etymological roots of the terms used in the two languages are not identical except in the case of *Verstand* and "understanding." "Intuition" and "reason" go back to the Romance (Norman) component of the English language, as most English abstract vocabulary does. But even "understanding" in its ambiguous grammatical form that causes in the user potential interference between the gerundial and progressive forms, is not such a close formal equivalent to the German as might be expected. *Das Verstehen,* the gerundial form (leaving the progressive form *verstehend* unconsidered in this case), is the equivalent nearest to "understanding." And yet, "intellect" is lurking as a tempting rendition in the back of the English translator's mind.

Terms from the Romance heritage of the English language are, characteristically, not terms of every-day common usage. They are generally terms of a more elevated, "highbrow" level of vocabulary, as it is indeed the case with "intuition" and "reason." The speaker of English using the term "intuition" is not immediately aware of the term's Latin root verb *intūeri* referring back to "looking at" by way of the senses. The English connotation of the noun "intuition" and of the verb "to intuit" is primarily "receiving knowledge" not so much through the senses but rather through a nondescript "hunch" emerging from the person's mental power and range of human experience.

As to "reason," the other term from the Romance heritage of English, we have a different problem linguistically. The term's general denotations of "ground," "cause," "statement of justification" interfere with the term's other denotational reference to the "mental powers which draw conclusions or inferences." While the historical development of the English language has removed the term's primary meaning from the connotation referring to the *activation* of mental activity (as the French *raisonner* still does) to the *completed product* of that mental activity, the "ground," or "cause" of a relationship, the general denotation now attached to "reason" as a philosophical term has become causal, stressing the result of mental activity in the sense of constituting permanent cause-effect relationships as they exist in the world of physics.

"Understanding," the third term under scrutiny, sharing its etymological root with the German verb *unterstehen* (which has undergone over the centuries drastic semantic change from "understanding" to "daring" or "venturing"), denotes in English the "perception of meaning" or the "grasping of the idea" with a strong underlying connotation of obtaining knowledge through "learning" or "hearing," which are both primarilily based on sensuous perception.

It is worthwhile to note in this context that all three terms are not words with which the speaker of English feels very comfortable. They are, at least in their philosophical sense, not words of frequent usage; they apparently contain connotations of too much abstraction and have, even in their more common everyday denotations, not found entry into the proverbial and idiomatic realms of the language. *Anschauung, Verstand,* and *Vernunft* have found, at least to some degree, their way into the proverbial and idiomatic usage of the German language, if not in their nominal form, then at least in a related conceptual version. Most revealing with respect to the semantic field of *Anschauung* is Goethe's poem "Lynkeus" with the lines *zum Sehen geboren / zum Schauen bestellt* (born to see / and ordered to observe). Here we find the fundamental differentiation between seeing (*Sehen*) and observing (*Schauen*) which reminds us of Vico's first book of the *Scienza Nuova* where the principles and methods of the "new science" rested on the unity of philosophy and philology and, among others, on the division between the old myths and newly invented interpretations of them. For Kant *Anschauung* is the simultaneous sensual awareness of the archetypal essence through the senses and not through the mind. It is seeing (*Sehen*) and observing (*Schauen*) in one. Seeing (*Sehen*) is used in the original sense of taking in the sights of the world via visual sense impression, whereas *Schauen* (observing) refers to a conscious perceiving of what is going on in actuality (and beyond because of its connotation with prophetical "seeing" as a means of relating to the transcendental). *Verstand* has become idiomatic in the saying *er hat seinen Verstand verloren* (he is out of his mind, has gone crazy), while *Vernunft* has found expression in *nimm doch Vernunft an* (please come to reason, come to your senses), which implies an expectation of acting reasonably.

The Old English term "inwit" meant literally "against reason" with the denotation of "evil," "deceitful behavior." A new formation of "inwit" during Middle English times associated its meaning with the moral conscience of a person as the "inward sense of right and wrong." Later semantic change developed the meaning of "wisdom" and "reason, intellect, understanding" for "inwit" as well as "heart, soul, mind" (*OED*). "Inwit" with its complex semantic field may be the only English term, obsolete as it may now be, which might capture the range of the Kantian *Anschauung*. But common usage has outwitted the philologist and translator since the word is no longer in common usage and, in addition, "inwit" has shed the "heart, soul, mind" connotation. The rationalists' denotation of "reason, intellect, understanding" has survived.

The key to a meaningful discussion of a philosophical translation

problem is the explanation of the epistemological schema that underlies a set of terms that has been semantically "loaded" beyond the
everyday usage of the individual term by the thoughts of the philosophical author in the attempt of developing and defining his contribution to the discipline. As the preceding discussion has shown, it
cannot be expected, even among closely related languages of the same
family, that terminological and full semantic equivalency can be obtained. History has modified these expectations not only on linguistic
and semantic grounds, but also on intellectual and cultural grounds
which direct a nation's traditions of thought according to different
premises.

> During the course of modern philosophy's epistemological investigations the
> tension between experience and philosophical speculation has been elevated
> into a polarizing internal philosophical strife between rationalists and em-
> piricists.[13]

A statement like this one clearly reflects the partiality of philosophical
movements and ideologies. Kant, through the experience of translators, is a case in point where not only the partiality and ideology of
different philosophical movements manifest themselves, but where it
is evident that even within the Western tradition there are fundamental differences of "seeing" the world which no longer can adequately
find equivalent expression in linguistic and semantic terms.

It would, therefore, be of little use to quibble with the tradition of
Kant translation which has pretty much established "intuition," "understanding," and "reason" as the English equivalents for the German
Anschauung, Verstand, and *Vernunft.* In his contribution to this volume
Professor Moltke Gram has already pointed to the philological and
philosophical damage inflicted by J. Hutchison Sterling, and a host
of others on consistent translation of Kant's *Anschauung.* The list of
offenders can easily be expanded to Carl J. Friedrich[14] and Gabriele
Rabel[15] who cannot resist to prefer "perception" over "intuition" on
different levels of sophistication. Furthermore, it is a characteristic
of the above Kant commentators, critics, and illuminators, but
generally not typical of translators, to play *va banque* with terminology.
Translators, apparently, do have a stronger awareness of the tradition of translation and, being aware of the quasi-equivalence of their
trade, will not engage in cosmetic correction of a semantically un-
solvable problem.

The most useful and constructive approach, without even having
to contend with the interpretation of these terms by competing

philosophical schools of thought, is to explain the semantic field of the author's terms and their place within the tradition. If this is successful, the reader of the translation only needs to be asked to read the text with caution and pay special attention to the meaning which the author attributes to a given term in his thought processes. When the reader is confronted with a philosophical text containing a still unfamiliar usage pattern, the reading has to be slow and meticulous, involving a weighing of words and meaning, because of the necessity of constantly absorbing the definitions which clarify the particular usage. What the reader in such a situation actually does is a voluntary opening of his mind to the semantically modified terminology which has been affected by the thought process of another mind or even a mind which has been formed by another culture, language, and tradition. The terminology used in the source language, as intentionally chosen by the author when he was constructing his thought, is the only terminology relevant to the grasping of the original semantic context since the unity of the linguistic and intellectual semantics is of primary importance.

The crucial point for the discovery of the meaning of *Anschauung* (intuition) is the definition of its place within the relevant history of philosophical thought. Even though "intuition" bears the mark of "spiritual perception or immediate knowledge, ascribed to angelic and spiritual beings, with whom vision and knowledge are identical" as defined by scholastic philosophy, later definitions of "intuition" remain associated with "immediate apprehension of an object by the mind" and "immediate apprehension by the intellect alone" (*OED*). Confusion as to definition and proper terminology is rampant. We are forced to take refuge in the specific philosopher and his system. Kant's meaning of *Anschauung* (intuition) hinges upon the interpretation of the ꞏrception of objects existing in this world through senses, particularly the sense of perceiving through vision (*anschauen*), which confronts eyes with objects or vice versa. The philosopher's question is concerned with how much, if any, of an object do we perceive through the senses? Do we intuitionally perceive all ingredients or qualities of an object at once like the sum total consisting of certain necessary units and other truths of fact based on direct "inner" experience (Leibniz)? Or, do we, with Locke, grant intuitive insight the highest degree of certainty in comparison to other modes of insight? In this tradition of interpreting "intuition," cognition is directly perceived on the basis of agreement or disagreement. It is "the eye of the understanding," says Locke, which directly perceives the truth by virtue of concentrating on that certain aspect which it is presently focusing on.   Intuitive cognition leads inevitably to the truth in the same way as sunshine forces itself with its brightness upon our eyes. The veracity of intuitive cognition could not be proven but also, *per definitionem,* would not be in need of proof since it is obvious that the circle is not a triangle.

Kant does not follow the traditional interpretation of "intuition." For him *Anschauung* (intuition) is a decidedly sense-related cognition which has close affinity to the image-related perceptive power of the imagination.   Consequently the stressing of the visual sense is etymologically closer to the literal meaning of *Anschauung* than to "intuition."   Kant's *cognitio sensitiva* (*Anschauung*) is a completely independent source of cognition.   It is of the same level of importance as *Verstand* (understanding).   In Kant's critical thinking *Anschauung* is the principle by which man perceives through senses.   *Anschauung* contains the manner in which, or better how, objects appear to us humans: *Anschauung* (intuition) does not ask for the cognition of the objects themselves since that question, in order to provide objectivity, is left to the understanding (*Verstand*).   *Anschauung* perceives or receives the objects within the dimensions of space and time through the senses and provides the objects for spontaneous action to the *Verstand* (understanding).   The multiplicity of independent *Anschauungen* (intuitions), meaning in this case "sense data," has already been perceived by *Anschauung* (intuition) before *Verstand* (understanding) begins its synthesis.   While *Anschauung* (intuition) "intuitively" *perceives* its object in its totality, *Verstand* (understanding) "discursively" arranges the parts of the object into a certain sequence so that a totality can be *constructed* on the basis of successive synthesis.

Space and time are the conditions for any human perception based on *Anschauung* and for any potential human cognition based on *Verstand.*   While space is the form and environment in which our "externally" perceptive sense functions, time is the manner and dimension in which the perceiving person as thinker "internalizes" or makes sense and use of the "sense data" provided by *Anschauung* (intuition).   Since time and space are continuous quantities (*quanta continua*) that do not constitute a unity composed of many parts, *Anschauung* (intuition) can never perform a cognitive function on the level of notions (*Begriffe*). There is no intuitive (*anschauende*) cognition of the world in its entirety, consequently there can neither be an "intellectual" *Anschauung* (intuition), nor an "intuitive" *Verstand* (understanding), at least for Kant, but not for Husserl.   "Intellectual" *Anschauung* is only possible as *intellectus archetypus* which would be representative of the divine intellect to whom his own creations would be self-evident.

While space and time are necessary conditions for "intuitively" perceiving objects through the senses via *Anschauung* (intuition), the four categories are the necessary conditions for "discursively" arranging the individual, experienced observations of the senses via the *Verstand* (understanding) into a unity. *Vernunft* (reason) as the highest power of human cognition, always intent on searching the systematic, i.e., the context that is affected by the principle, is only occupied with itself because it is working exclusively with results of the *Verstand*'s (understanding's) cognition pertaining to the assumed unity of the system. *Vernunft* (reason) does neither operate on the basis of space and time, nor on the basis of categories. It makes use of cognition arranged by *Verstand* (understanding) in an unsensuous and nonempirical way by considering its business according to *ideas* (*Ideen*) instead of categories or space and time. *Vernunft* (reason) operates on the basis of freedom. It not only transcends the sense data supplied by *Anschauung* (intuition) but also sits in judgment over the activities of *Anschauung* and *Verstand*. It is the task of *Vernunft* (reason) to investigate all possible principles of unity. Its only natural limit of operation is the range of potential human experience. *Vernunft* (reason) as the fountain of ideas, however, cannot and will not make judgments without notions (*Begriffe*) of *Verstand* (understanding). Countering Leibniz, Kant says that symbolic cognition, which is characteristic of *Vernunft* (reason), is ultimately an intuitive cognition because the idea of *Vernunft* (reason) necessarily refers back to *Anschauung* (intuition).

Kant's epistemological paradigm as it reveals itself through *Anschauung, Verstand,* and *Vernunft* is, of course, typical of the philosophical movement that has come to be known as German Idealism. Its terminology and principles of thought structure are as *sui generis* as those of other philosophical movements. And yet, a translation, a literal "carrying over" of terminology, paradigms, and basic axioms into English is so much more difficult than one would expect since the traditions of Idealism in Germany and Pragmatism in England have developed the philosophical thought process in both languages and cultures along different lines. Consequently, a translator can only rely on words that refer to the basic concept germane to the general and shared tradition of Western philosophy and leave the rest of the work of understanding to the reader. Any unique modification of linguistic and semantic concepts has to be left to the particular explanation of the individual philosopher who has authored these modifications because in such a redefinition of the tradition lies his creativity and professional stature. The translator, even though he is "only" dealing in words, cannot treat cognition as behaviorists do. The translator can only be an honest mediator, he must understand the subject he is translating, but he can neither alter the languages he is working with, nor the intellectual contents of his subject, nor is he allowed to inject his own opinion into the material.

> From the perspective of the history of the problem and from the perspective of systematics transcendental philosophy is of special importance to the discussion and definition of the relation between experience, the theory of experience, and philosophical speculation.[16]

For the translator, however, it will have to suffice to inform the reader within the confines of the target language of Kant's revolutionary "Copernican Reversal," which abolished the dependence of consciousness from objects and instead posited the objects' dependence on the *a priori* structure of human consciousness. Whether such information about a philosophical concept should be interpreted as a catching up with Hume's empiricism and Newton's physics, or whether it should be interpreted as an incorporation of empericism into a more comprehensive universal system of philosophy, must be left to the reader while the terminology used in the translation and the faithful rendering of the philosophical context offered by the translator should make such judgment possible.

One last and final point must still be made when translation in the context of Kantian philosophy is discussed. At the very end, in the next to the last sentence, of the *Critique of Pure Reason,* Kant made a very important statement relevant to the understanding of his philosophy of *Kritizismus.* He said that "the critical path is the only one which is still open."[17] This crucial statement contains the very essence of Kantian thinking. It is a statement stressing the open-endedness of all thinking and interpretations. In our unending struggles with the meaning of this world, we are constantly developing interpretations (*doxa*) along the lines of insight generated from theoretical (*theoria*) and/or empirical (*praxis*) grounds. We are pretending also that we are attributing the status of a dogmatic truth to these interpretations. However, Kant warns that such interpretation can become dogma or ideology since this would run absolutely contrary to the dynamics and creativity of human cultural activity. This Kantian statement also holds true for the art of translation and its interpretation of meaning. The interpretative circle of meaning, as far as translation is concerned, begins with the author who turns his insight into a text which undergoes its first interpretation as trans-lation (carrying-over) and closes with the second interpretation performed by the individual reader of that translation. The critical path remains thereby open because interpretations will on both levels necessarily vary within reasonable limits, depending on perspective and power of thought, whereas the original text still remains an intentional object created by its author.[18]

NOTES

1   Ernst Cassirer, ed., *Immanuel Kants Werke* (Berlin: Cassirer, 1912-22), vol. 11, p. 92.

2   Hilaire Belloc, *On Translation,* Taylorian Lecture, 1931 (Oxford: Clarendon Press, 1931). In an essay "On Translation" Belloc describes the plight of the translator as follows: "It is true that the heaven-born translator, like the heaven-born poet, can be bought cheap sometimes and starved to death." *A Conversation with an Angel* (New York: Harper, 1929), p. 150.

3   Edward Sapir, *Culture, Language and Personality* (Berkeley, Los Angeles: University of California Press, 1956), p. 69.

4   *Immanuel Kant's Critique of Pure Reason,* trans. by Norman Kemp Smith (New York: St. Martin's Press, 1963), p. v.

5   Ibid.

6   Ibid.

7   I am using the rather recent term "translation studies" as used in one of the most important publications on *Literature and Translation,* ed. by Holmes, Lambert, and van den Broeck, ACCO (Leuven, 1978).

8   *Academy 2* (August 1890), pp. 278-79.

9   Matthew Arnold, "On Translating Homer," Lecture 1, in *Essays by Matthew Arnold,* (London: Oxford University Press, 1914), p. 247.

10   Quoted in William J. De Sua, *Dante into English* (Chapel Hill: University of North Carolina Press, 1964), p. 65.

11   See also Susan Bassnett-McGuire, *Translation Studies* (New York: Methuen, 1980), p. 68ff.

12   For a more detailed investigation of past renderings of Kant's *Anschauung* into English and the ensuing philosophical implications, see Professor Moltke Gram's contribution to this volume.

13   Helmut Fahrenbach, "Erfahrung und Sprache in philosophischer Reflexion," in *Sprache und Welterfahrung,* ed. by Jörg Zimmermann (Munich: Fink, 1978), p. 20. (The translation is mine.)

14   Cf. Carl J. Friedrich, ed., *The Philosophy of Kant* (New York: Random House, 1949), pp. xxx-xxxii.

15   Cf. Gabriele Rabel, *Kant* (Oxford: Clarendon Press, 1963), pp. xiv-xv.

16   Fahrenbach, p. 20. (The translation is mine.)

17   The English translation is mine. Kant's original reads: "der kritische Weg ist allein noch offen."

18   For a detailed explanation of the artwork as an "international object" within the stratum of meaning units, see Roman Ingarden, *The Literary Work of Art,* trans. by G. Grabowicz (Evanston: Northwestern University Press, 1973), pp. 118-19. For the most comprehensive recent study of Ingarden's literary theory see Eugene H. Falk, *The Poetics of Roman Ingarden* (Chapel Hill: University of North Carolina Press, 1981), particularly pp. 37-40.

HANS SEIGFRIED

Kant's "Spanish Bank Account": *Realität* and *Wirklichkeit*

More is needed than a linguistically accurate translation in order to make Kant's writings fully accessible to Anglo-American philosophers who come from a different tradition than the one in which Kant wrote; the tradition in which and against which Kant was writing has to be made accessible as well. Like the more general need to read Kant's writings *entwicklungsgeschichtlich*,[1] so this more particular need, too, has been recognized relatively late.[2]

Kant wrote in the tradition of the German university- or school-philosophy.[3] Although the influences of Plato, Aristotle, Descartes, and Leibniz are as much felt in Anglo-American philosophy as in German school-philosophy, the influences of Spanish scholasticism, of Suarez in particular,[4] and of Christian Wolff are peculiar to the German tradition. Some important ideas in Kant's *Critique of Pure Reason* and other writings that cause considerable difficulty for Anglo-American philosophers are easily understood when seen in this context. I shall try to demonstrate this point with regard to the distinction between *Realität* and *Wirklichkeit,* or, more generally, with regard to Kant's discovery of the peculiarity of the categories of modality.

It strikes me as odd that such a competent translator as N. K. Smith, in his mostly reliable translation of the *Critique of Pure Reason,*[5] is not always faithful to Kant's use of the words *real/Realität* and *wirklich/ Wirklichkeit.* As I have pointed out elsewhere,[6] he renders, for example,

Hans Seigfried is professor of philosophy, Loyola University of Chicago, Chicago, Illinois.

wirklich/Wirklichkeit in such passages as B266 and B288 (footnote) correctly as "actual/actuality." Even in the well-known passage B626ff he translates *Wirklichkeit* as "actuality" and *real/Realität* as real/reality." Only when it comes to Kant's "bank account" and to the explicit comparison between *das Wirkliche* and *das Mögliche,* between a hundred *wirklichen Thalern* and a hundred *möglichen Thalern* does he surprisingly change his practice and translate *das Wirkliche* as "the real" and *wirkliche Thaler* as "real thalers." Afterwards, on the same page, he translates *Wirklichkeit* again as "actuality."

In this passage, however, Kant is not comparing the possible with the real, as Smith would have it, but with the actual, and he claims that there is absolutely no difference between the actual and the possible in respect to reality — both are equally real. Smith, accordingly, confuses Kant's point of comparison (as do J. M. D. Meiklejohn and M. Müller in their translations of this passage).[7] Surely Kant would object that Smith's practice robs him of his actual savings, and he would complain that the hundred real thalers Smith leaves him are nothing the mere concept of his savings, now lost due to Smith's negligence. He would never agree to what Smith assures him of, namely, that his bank account is "affected very differently by a hundred real thalers than it is by the mere concept of them (that is, of their possibility)."[8] Instead, Kant would stubbornly maintain that only a hundred actual thalers would make a difference.

Even Professor L. W. Beck occasionally confuses *Realität* and *Wirklichkeit,* for instance, in his remarks on Kant's criticism of Crusius and of the classical ontological argument for the existence of God. In his review of Crusius' "new laws of thought," Professor Beck refers to Kant's objections to the principle that "I *cannot think* of a thing as existing without thinking that it is somewhere and at some time."[9] Professor Beck claims that in *The Only Premise for a Demonstration of the Existence of God*[10] "Kant objects that this principle does not distinguish between real and possible objects."[11] It seems to me, however, that Kant's criticism is not quite concerned with the distinction between reality and possibility, but rather between actuality or existence and possibility, on the one side, and something *toto genere* different, namely, reality, on the other side. For what Kant objects to is Crusius' claim that "some-where" and "some-when" are determinations of actuality or existence (*Bestimmungen des Daseins*), such that they could be used as criteria for distinguishing what actually exists from what is merely possible. Against this claim Kant argues that these "predicates" cannot possibly determine things, insofar as they actually exist (*wirklich da* [*sind*]), because they determine things which are merely possible, and which do not actually exist (*wirklich nicht da* [*sind*]), as well.[12] They are predicates which merely determine what a thing and its reality consist in, and not at all whether a thing could, actually does, or must exist.

And in his discussion of Kant's critique of the ontological argument, Professor Beck points out that Kant recognized already in *The Only Premise* the crucial error in the classical argument by realizing "that existence is not a predicate, and hence the existence of a thing cannot be inferred from concepts alone."[13] Kant's critique, he says, remains basically the same in the *Critique of Pure Reason,* except that "the modal concepts of possibility, *reality,* and necessity" lose their "ontological significance" and retain only their "regulative significance in the organization of experience."[14]

But it seems to me that Kant does not hold, as I will try to show below, that existence is not a predicate, but merely that it is not "a predicate or determination of any thing (*von irgend einem Dinge*)," "of the thing itself (*von dem Dinge selbst*),"[15] or, in short, that it is not a *real* predicate in a rather technical sense.[16] After all, in the *Critique of Pure Reason* Kant leaves no doubt that all categories of modality *are* predicates,[17] they are just not *real* predicates, because "in determining the object, they do not in the least enlarge the concept to which they are attached as predicates,"[18] i.e., "no additional determinations are thereby thought *in the object itself.*"[19] However, what strikes me more is that Professor Beck lists *reality* in place of actuality as the second category of modality. For surely Professor Beck knows that in the *Critique of Pure Reason* reality belongs to the categories of quality, and not to the categories of modality.

My reason for pointing out these errors is not to draw attention to mistakes, though mistakes they are, but rather to indicate that the Kantian distinction between *Realität* and *Wirklichkeit* is so foreign to Anglo-American philosophers — and to contemporary German philosophers as well — that even the best blur it, or overlook it altogether, the moment they are not fully on guard.[20] We must continuously remind ourselves of that distinction and of its importance, because ordinarily we do not distinguish in English — or in contemporary German — between reality and actuality, at least not as drastically as does Kant. He insists that reality and actuality are different in kind, and not only in degree, as an old tradition has it. This tradition is represented best, for Kant at least, by Christian Wolff and Alexander Gottlieb Baumgarten, and the rare exception to it by Franciscus

Suarez — although Kant nowhere indicates, to my knowledge, that he knew him directly.[21] In order to more adequately understand Kant's distinction and to appreciate its importance and significance, we need to know the long and troubled tradition to which Kant's distinction is meant to put an end. A brief review of Kant's claims concerning this distinction, and a brief contrast of them with those found in Wolff and Baumgarten is in order.

Kant claims that being (*Sein, Dasein, Existenz, Wirklichkeit*) is obviously not a *real* predicate or (a predicate which stands for) something real that could be added to the thing itself. Rather, it is merely the positing of the thing itself *in itself,* or of some of its properties (*Bestimmungen, Merkmale*) *in themselves,* that is, "outside their concepts."[22]

Interpreters frequently complain that Kant's notion of a real predicate is obscure.[23] However, if they would bother to study the tradition from which Kant inherited the notion of being as a real predicate, instead of merely speculating about it, they would easily and clearly realize that what Kant *rejects* is an old and quite simple understanding of being and existence according to which we accept as fully, completely, and perfectly real what is actually there and exists in itself. Adding, so to speak, existence and actuality to something that is a merely possible thing, or property, increases and completes its reality such that it becomes something that is fully real, i.e., a thing, or a property, which actually exists in itself.

In somewhat elaborate form, this understanding of existence and actuality is the doctrine of nearly all "old students of Thomas Aquinas," as Suarez points out in his *Disputationes metaphysicae* (1597).[24] According to his review,[25] the doctrine suggests that the reality of an actually existing thing (*ens existens*) is composed of two "elements," namely, existence and essence, which differ from each other *ex natura rei,* or as two things (*res*) differ from each other, such that one represents the actuality and the other the possibility of a thing. Accordingly, if something is fully determined as a real or as a complete thing (*res*), then it must exist. Suarez criticizes and rejects this doctrine, as does Kant, although ultimately for radically different reasons.[26] Despite the great influence of Suarez on German school-philosophy, the doctrine survives somehow, and we still find it in the writings of Wolff and Baumgarten and, beyond Kant, in the writings of more recent students of Thomas Aquinas.[27]

Against this "old" doctrine," Suarez points out, as does Kant, that it certainly does not follow from the fact that something is fully determined as real, or as a certain kind of thing (*res*), that it also exists, still less that it exists necessarily.[28] And this is so because being is not a predicate, or a determination, of a thing, or, as Suarez puts it, because existence does not belong to the *predicaments,* or categories, which determine merely what kind of a *thing* is, i.e., its *quidditas,* thingness, or reality. For even complete *predicamental* determination cannot furnish a thing with actuality or existence.[29] And this is what the first and negative part of Kant's thesis about being states.

Kant admits that his claim that being is not a predicate, or determination, of a thing sounds odd and meaningless, but he insists that it is nevertheless justified for obvious reasons, such as the following. If we conceive of a thing, together with some or all of its predicates, then "we do not make the least addition to the thing when we further declare that this thing *is.* Otherwise it would not be exactly the same thing that exists, but something more than we had thought in the concept; and we could not, therefore, say [as we obviously can] that the exact object of my concept exists."[30] Suarez gives a similar argument against the alleged additive character of existence.[31]

However, Kant does not claim, as is sometimes assumed, that being is not a predicate at all.[32] In *The Only Premise* and in the *Critique of Pure Reason* he argues only that it cannot be a predicate of the thing itself, or a *real* predicate. But in the earlier work he admits and emphasizes that in ordinary languge existence can safely and correctly (*sicher und ohne besorglich Irrthümer*) be used as a predicate. For instance, we can meaningfully say that the sea unicorn exists and the land unicorn does not exist. Kant believes that this is so because ordinarily (except for those rare occasions of abstract thinking, for instance, about God as an absolutely necessary being) we use being not as a predicate of *the thing itself* but as a predicate of *the concept of the thing* instead, or, if you permit a slight extension of his terminology, as a *conceptual* predicate. As such a predicate it determines and qualifies not the thing itself or *what* we think the thing to be, but the concept of the thing, namely, as a concept of a thing which exists in nature or is contained within the context of experience. In other words, it qualifies the concept of the thing as a concept of experience (*Erfahrungsbegriff*). What we must mean, then, when we say that the sea unicorn exists, is that the concept of a sea unicorn is the concept of a thing which exists, or, more accurately, that all the predicates and attributes which we conceive as the predicates of a unicorn in our concept of a unicorn can be found in an existing sea animal.[33]

Clearly then for Kant existence is a *conceptual* predicate, i.e., a predicate which qualifies our concept of a thing. However, it is not a *real* predicate in a technical sense such that it does not determine the thing itself and its thingness or reality which we conceive in our concepts. But being is also positing, or position (*Position, Setzung*), as the second and positive part of Kant's thesis about being states. And as *positing* it is neither a purely conceptual nor a real predicate. For as positing it adds nothing to the thing itself nor does it qualify merely and simply our concept of it. If, in view of Kant's remarks on the peculiarity of the categories of modality, one wants to call existence as position a predicate, then one must point out that it is a very peculiar predicate, indeed.

Positing can be logical, i.e., relative, and absolute. Logically, being as positing is a merely *relative* positing because "the small word 'is' [in a judgment such as 'God is omnipotent'] adds no new predicate, but only serves to posit the predicate *in its relation* to the subject."[34] And as the positing of this relation (called *respectus logicus*),[35] being is "merely the copula of a judgment,"[36] i.e., it is "nothing but the conceptual connection (*Verbindungsbegriff*) in a judgment."[37] Of course, as the positing of a relation between concepts, logical positing does not signify the being of a thing, i.e., actuality (*Dasein, Wirklichkeit*) in the sense of the second category of modality.[38] For Kant, only the *absolute* positing of the thing itself can signify being or existence in that sense, where by absolute positing he means the positing of the thing itself (or, of the thing itself together with some or all of its properties and predicates) *in itself* (*an und fuer sich selbst*),[39] "outside of the concepts,"[40] in nature,[41] and as contained within the context of experience.[42]

Kant gives this explanation of existence already in *The Only Premise*. The frequent references in my description to the *Critique of Pure Reason* should not obscure this fact. However, much more clarification is needed. The relationship between the absolute positing, our concepts, and our experience of the thing is still much too vague for a clear distinction both between its reality and actuality, and its possibility, actuality, and necessity. A satisfactory clarification of these relations is accomplished only in the much broader context of the *Critique of Pure Reason*. For the purposes of this paper, a brief indication of these needs and accomplishments must suffice.

It turns out that not only the positing of the thing itself, as such, but also the absolute positing of the thing itself in itself cannot precisely represent for Kant actuality in the sense of the second category of modality. For the explanation of the categories of modality and the postulates of empirical thought in general show that the positing of the thing itself, for instance, in relation to both intuition (*Anschauung*) and the understanding and its synthesis, within the transcendental unity of apperception and transcendental self-consciousness, does not signify actuality, but merely the possibility of the thing as conceived in and through such synthesis, i.e., the first category of modality.[43] And in order for the absolute position of the thing itself in itself and "outside the concepts" to signify precisely the second category of modality, the defining characteristics of the absolute position must be understood more specifically, namely, the "outside the concepts" as outside intuition and the understanding and its synthesis, and the "in itself" as in, or "inside," perception (*Wahrnehmung*) and sensation (*Empfindung*).[44]

Of course, in the positing of the thing itself through the understand- and its synthesis alone, the thing gets determined only through the pure concepts of the understanding, i.e., the categories (except for the categories of modality, of course). For instance, by positing something in the thing as substance or subject, all the other "elements" or "realities" in the thing are rendered as predicates, attributes, or determinations which, through subsequent synthesis, have to be added on to the subject such that together they constitute *what* the thing is in its entirety. But clearly such categorial synthesis alone, by merely putting together everything which belongs to the thingness or reality of a thing, can never render a thing as belonging directly or indirectly to the context of experience, as actually existing in nature, or "outside the concepts" — unless, of course, such existence is presupposed all along. In accordance with the law of (non-)contradiction alone, it merely posits relations in the thing itself, namely, those between the subject and its predicates.[45] And as such a synthetic and *a priori* positing of the thing itself, i.e., without reference to intuition, perception and sensation, and the universal conditions of experience in general, it cannot show (*belegen*) anything whatsoever about the "real" possibility, the actual existence, or the necessary existence of the thing itself.[46] As Kant puts it, "it is not . . . surprising that, if we attempt to think existence through the pure category alone, we cannot specify a single mark distinguishing it from mere possibility."[47] The successful synthesis of the thingness or reality of a thing, in accordance with the law of (non-)contradiction — even its *complete* synthesis such that "in my concept nothing may be lacking of the possible real content of a thing at all"[48] — demonstrates only the *a priori*, inner, or mere possibility of a thing, i.e., it shows only *what* we conceive a thing to be can be conceived without contradiction. It does not, and it cannot, show by itself that "this object is also possible *a posteriori*," namely, as an object of experience.[49] The reality of a thing, as such, remains therefore a purely *conceptual* matter.

How the mere reality and inner possibility of a thing can be distinguished from both the "real" possibility and the actuality of an object of experience, Kant shows in his exposition of "The Postulates of Empirical Thought in General," i.e., in his explanation of the categories of modality.[50] He claims that in order for the conceptual reality of a thing to be the reality of a *possible* object of experience, the thing has to be posited also in accordance "with the formal conditions of experience, that is, with the conditions of intuition and of concepts."[51] And in order for it to be the reality of an *actual* object of experience, it has to be posited as "bound up with the material conditions of experience, that is, with sensation," as well.[52]

In the explanation which follows his statement of the postulates or principles of modality, Kant insists that "the categories of modality have the peculiarity" that they are predicates which "do not in the least enlarge" the concept to which they are attached as determinations of a thing.[53] They add no further determinations "in the object,"[54] and they play no part in the conceptual synthesis of the thingness or reality of a thing, or, as Kant puts it, they are not "objectively synthetic," because they "do not in the least" add to "the representation of the object."[55] They are "synthetic . . . subjectively only, that is, they add to the concept of a thing (of something *real*) . . . the cognitive faculty from which it springs and in which it has its seat."[56] In short, they add nothing to the reality of a thing, that is, to *what* we conceive a thing to be. But they do add to the concept of a thing the relation to "the cognitive faculty," or, to put it the other way around and more accurately, they add the conceptual reality of a thing to the objects of experience.[57]

Consequently, it seems to me that there can be no doubt that Kant holds that being or existence, as position, is a predicate after all. It is a highly specific *conceptual* predicate, i.e., a predicate which qualifies the *concept* of a thing, specifically, as being in conformity with the formal conditions of experience such that it is directly or indirectly connected (in accordance with the analogies of experience, and with the laws of the empirical connection of appearances) to the *actual* perception and sensation of the thing itself,[58] i.e., to the thing as it is "given absolutely" and *a posteriori*.[59] However, being is not a *real* predicate in the technical sense explained. It adds nothing to the thingness or reality of a thing. Kant's strong insistence on this point ("do not in the least"), both at the outset and at the end of his explanation of the peculiarity of the categories of modality in the *Critique of Pure Reason,* indicates that he saw his explanation both as a refutation of a highly regarded old doctrine and as a central piece in his revolutionary philosophy.

In *The Only Premise,* after summing up in two sentences[60] the first exposition of the nucleus of this explanation of existence, in its difference from reality, Kant points out, so to speak as an afterthought, that his explanation as a matter of course grew out of both his unprejudiced reading and his critical appropriation of what his predecessors had written on the subject. But he assumes that his readers are still sufficiently familiar with the old doctrine to judge easily for themselves what is new in his explanation and what deviates from the tradition, and how it does so. And that is why it was not his intention to present an explicit and detailed refutation of it. Since he is writing for such informed readers, a few hints would suffice. And so Kant barely mentions the relevant claims affected by his new explanation in the writings of Wolff, Baumgarten, and Crusius.[61]

But it seems to me that these hints no longer suffice for today's readers, for Anglo-American readers in particular, as demonstrated by the difficulties described above, which English translators have with Kant's "bank account." Naturally, Kant's whole discussion of existence and reality, both in the formulation of its problem and in the argumentation for the solution proposed, must appear to be "all Greek," or "Spanish" as the German saying goes, to readers who are not familiar with the tradition which Kant's explanation was meant to end, or who come from a different tradition altogether. And this is most naturally so when in their attempts to understand Kant's explanation they ignore the hints given, and all too eagerly follow up some ideas that Russell and G. E. Moore put forward instead. I feel that much confusion could be avoided if we would try to grasp Kant's explanation in its own historical context first before we follow up more recent ideas, as we ultimately should.

Kant claims it to be obvious that Wolff's definition of the existence of a thing as the perfection or complement (*Ergänzung*) of its possibility is very hazy, unless one knows already what possibility is.[62] But, instead of recalling and discussing at this point Wolff's notion of possibility, he reviews Baumgarten's notion of existence and possibility. Of course, Kant does not mean to suggest that Wolff of all people does not define possibility. Rather, he assumes both that the reader is sufficiently familiar with Wolff's notions and that he realizes that

Baumgarten's definitions are basically the same, except that they are more developed and, consequently, better fit for the discussion. Before reviewing his criticism, let me briefly recall Wolff's definition of possibility as well as his definitions of other notions central to the discussion of the distinction between reality and actuality.

In his *Philosophia prima sive Ontologia* (1730), Wolff claims that something is something *possible* (*possibile*) if it is not impossible, that is, if it does not involve a contradiction. [63] For in order to be a something (*aliquid*) at all, it has to be thought at least, and a something that involves a contradiction cannot even be thought[64] and is, consequently, nothing at all (*nihil*).[65] A triangle, for instance, is a something because space limited by three straight lines can be thought without contradiction.[66] Thus, to be a something (*aliquid*) at all or to be some "what" (*aliud quid*),[67] means to be a possible something, which in turn means to be a possible thought. And this is why Wolff can claim, in full agreement with the scholastics and tradition, as he points out, that whatever is, as well as whatever can simply be thought (to be possible) at all, is a thing (*res*). After all, a thing is a thing simply because it is a something.[68] And this explains for Wolff why one can use the term "reality" (*realitas*) as a synonym for "quiddity" (*quidditas*), or why the term "res" can be used as a "quidditative" predicate, as Suarez puts it succinctly, attributing the idea to de Soto, Thomas Aquinas, and Avicenna.[69] A tree, for instance, Wolff explains, can be taken as an entity (*ens*), i.e., as something which actually exists, and as a mere thing (*res*). If we talk about it as a thing, then we are talking merely about its quiddity, i.e., we are talking about it as a mere something that can be thought in a definite way, and we thereby completely ignore that it is also something that actually exists, if indeed it actually exists. [70]

However, Suarez, whose influence was mainly responsible for the survival of this scholastic terminology in German school-philosophy,[71] warned—in vain—that if we want to make such a technical, terminological distinction between *"res"* and *"ens"* (and we could add, between "reality" and "actuality"), then we have to keep reminding ourselves of the distinction to avoid confusion, for we must realize that these terms are used as synonyms in ordinary language.[72]

It seems to be clear from these considerations that possibility and reality are conceptually the same for Wolff. Both mean the thingness, whatness, or essence of a thing, insofar as it is merely conceptually or logically possible, insofar as it can be thought without contradiction. Reality in this technical sense is, consequently, conceptually different from actuality or existence, for it seems to be obvious that if something is possible, it does not thereby exist.[73] Houses and machines, for instance, are not actually built merely by designing them and by realizing that they can be built. In order for what actually exists (*ens*) to exist, Wolff argues, something else (*aluid quid*) is required, in addition to its possibility.[74] For if nothing else would be required, then it would follow that what actually exists, exists because it is merely possible; in other words, that mere possibility is a sufficient reason for existence, is absurd.[75] And this is why Wolff defines existence, or actuality, as the complement of possibility (*complementum possibilitatis*).[76] It is something that must be *added* to the mere possibility of what actually exists in order to *complete* its mere possibility and to transport it into actuality. What that is, Wolff seems to suggest, cannot be said in general.[77]

It appears that Baumgarten, in his *Metaphysica* (1739),[78] is making up for this shortcoming of Wolff's definition of existence. According to Baumgarten, existence, as the complement of the essence or inner possibility of a thing, must be understood more specifically as the complex of all those internal determinations within something (*in aliquo*) which are compatible with each other.[79] Of course, what is merely possible is a complex of some such determinations also; after all, such determinations make up the essence or inner possibility of a thing, and what lacks them altogether is simply nothing (*nihil negativum*).[80] However, what actually exists (*ens*) is made up of additional such determinations, beyond those which make up its essence or inner possibility; to be precise, it is made up of *all* the determinations which are compatible with each other within what actually exists.[81] Existence then completes what is merely possible by complementing its essential determinations.

For Baumgarten, however, all such determinations, or predicates, are realities. Whatever is posited within something as a positive or affirmative determination is a reality, he claims.[82] What remained obscure in Wolff's explanation thus seems to become clear, namely, that some other *realities* (in fact, *all* the realities which are compatible with those realities which make up the essence or inner possibility of a thing) have to be added to the mere possibility of what actually exists in order to complete it and to transport it into actuality. Existence itself turns out to be a reality,[83] or a *real* predicate, consisting of all the complementary realities still lacking in the merely possible. In short, the difference between mere possibility and actuality is a difference in the degree of reality or real determination.

Clearly, Baumgarten's explanation of existence is a mere variation of the old doctrine, described above, which Suarez attributes to
nearly all the "old students of Thomas Aquinas," and a simplistic
variation at that, compared with Suarez's sophisticated reconstruction.
But Kant had high regard for Baumgarten and "regularly used his
Metaphysica as a textbook in his lectures."[84] The idea of being as a
real predicate, which Kant so emphatically rejects in the critical and
negative part of his thesis about being, is then clearly not a hazy idea
whose exact meaning must forever escape us, or which we can best
reconstruct by following up more recent ideas about predication. I
have tried to show that it is quite an old idea, and that Kant rejects
it exactly in the form which Wolff and, ultimately, Baumgarten, for
better or worse, had given to it. In *The Only Premise* it is explicitly re-
called as Baumgarten's idea, namely, as the claim that it is the complete inner determination (*die durchgaengige innere Bestimmung*) of a thing
which constitutes the difference between its actuality and its mere
possibility.[85] Kant claims that his deliberations have shown that the
mere connection of a thing with all possible, i.e., conceivable (*erdenk-
lichen*) predicates can never transport it from mere possibility to actuality.[86] The same point is then repeated, without mention of Baumgarten, in the *Critique of Pure Reason*.[87] To Baumgarten's idea, Kant
objects that adding real predicates or realities accomplishes nothing
with regard to possibility and actuality because the difference between
them is not a difference in the amount of reality at all.

Kant was not the first to make this point. In view of his explanation
of existence, Suarez could have insisted likewise that a hundred possible dollars, merely conceived, was exactly the same amount as a
hundred actual dollars, although in his Spanish "bank account" a
hundred possible dollars plus a hundred actual dollars, unfortunately,
would not add up to two hundred dollars.[88]

Although I cannot remove all doubts about Suarez's "bank account"
at this point, I hope that I have shown that the troubles of Anglo-
American philosophers with Kant's "bank account," described earlier,
are due not so much to a lack of solid knowledge of German as to a
lack of familiarity with Kant's philosophical environment and, even
more so, to our strong absorption in contemporary philosophical
discussions. In conclusion, I would like to submit that more is needed
than a linguistically accurate translation in order to make Kant's
writings fully accessible in a foreign language and in a philosophically
different environment.

NOTES

1   Without de-emphasizing what was new and revolutionary in Kant's work, only in our time have some tried to show how Kant's writings emerged from an intensive discussion of the central problems of traditional philosophy and led, through a "living renewal" (G. Martin) of the old ontology, to new developments. See, among others, G. Martin, *Kant's Metaphysics and Theory of Science,* trans. by P. G. Lucas, 2nd ed. (Manchester: Manchester University Press, 1961); H. J. de Vleeschauwer, "Wie ich jetzt die Kritik der reinen Vernunft entwicklungsgeschichtlich lese," *Kant-Studien,* 54 (1963), pp. 351-63; and, above all, G. Tonelli, in the context of this paper, especially "Das Wiederaufleben der deutsch-aristotelischen Terminologie bei Kant," *Archiv für Begriffsgeschichte,* 9 (1964), pp. 223-42.

2   The best that has been done so far to meet this need is, of course, L. W. Beck, *Early German Philosophy: Kant and His Predecessors* (Cambridge: Harvard University Press, 1969). To get an idea of how little had been done in English before, see the final section, "An Informal Bibliography," pp. 505-39.

3   By German school-philosophy I mean the tradition of the academic philosophy at German universities, particularly the academic philosophy both in the Age of Orthodoxy, known as Protestant scholasticism, and in the Age of Enlightenment. For an excellent introduction, see L. W. Beck, *Early German Philosophy,* especially the sections on "Nominalism and the Rise of University-Philosophy," pp. 72-82, "Scholasticism in the Age of Orthodoxy," pp. 122-31, and the introduction to "Two Founders of the German Enlightenment," pp. 243-47.

4   Ibid., pp. 122-23. Kant's fondness for "schulgerechte Pünktlichkeit" is notorious. I think that it is enlightening in this context to read his remark about "die strengsten Regeln einer schulgerechten Puenktlichkeit" (*Prolegomena, Akademie Ausgabe,* vol. 4, p. 261), together with Goethe's characterization of the rules of Logic as "Spanish boots." See J. W. Goethe, *Faust,* trans. by W. Kaufmann (New York: Doubleday Anchor, 1961), p. 199. All German texts from Kant's writings used in this paper are from the *Akademie Ausgabe, Kants gesammelte Schriften,* ed. by the Prussian Academy of Science (Berlin: Walter de Gruyter, 1902/12).

5   I. Kant, *Critique of Pure Reason,* trans. by N. K. Smith (New York: St. Martin's, 1965). *Kritik der reinen Vernunft,* 2nd or B ed., *Akademie Ausgabe,* vol. 3.

6   See my paper, "Kant's Thesis About Being Anticipated by Suarez?" in *Proceedings of the Third International Kant Congress,* ed. by L. W. Beck (Dordrecht: D. Reidel, 1972), pp. 518-19 n. 6.

7   See I. Kant, *Critique of Pure Reason,* 1st ed., 1860, trans. by J. M. D. Meiklejohn (New York: Dutton, 1946), p. 350, and I. Kant, *Critique of Pure Reason,* 1st ed., 1881, trans. by F. M. Mueller (New York: Macmillan, 1896), p. 483.

8   I. Kant, *Critique of Pure Reason,* B627.

9   L. W. Beck, *Early German Philosophy,* p. 397-98.

10   I. Kant, *Der einzig mögliche Beweisgrund zu einer Demonstration des Daseins Gottes, Akademie Ausgabe,* vol. 2, pp. 76-77 (Thereafter *Beweisgrund*).

11   L. W. Beck, *Early German Philosophy*, p. 398 n. 11.

12   I. Kant, *Beweisgrund*, p. 76.

13   L. W. Beck, *Early German Philosophy*, p. 454.

14   Ibid., p. 455 (emphasis added).

15   I. Kant, *Beweisgrund*, p. 72. See also *Kritik der reinen Vernunft*, B626.

16   I. Kant, *Kritik der reinen Vernunft*, B626.

17   Ibid., B266. In a recent paper, "Kant on Existence, Predication, and the Onto-logical Argument," *Dialectica*, 35 (1981), pp. 127-46, Professor J. Hintikka claims that "Kant maintains that none of the modal categories is a predicate" (p. 145 n. 28). Professor Hintikka is obviously mistaken. But such mistakes are unavoidable if one tries to come to terms with Kant's claims about existence as a predicate without ap-preciating his subtle technical distinctions, discussed below. The fact that these distinctions were already pointed out to Professor Hintikka some time ago merely proves how difficult it is to grasp them. See H. Wagner, "Über Kants Satz, das Dasein sei kein Prädikat," in *Archiv fuer Geschichte der Philosophie*, 53 (1971), pp. 183-86.

18   Ibid. See also B287.

19   Ibid. (emphasis added). W. Roed claims that the category of existence is con-ceptually different from the ontological determination of existence as the absolute position of a thing which has nothing to do with the conditions of the predication of existence (*Wirklichkeitsprädikation*), as does the modal category of existence and the second postulate of empirical thought in general. See W. Roed, "Die Bedeutung von 'Wirklichkeit' in Kants Theorie der Erfahrung," in *Akten des 4. Internationalen Kant-Kongresses*, Teil II.1, ed. by G. Funke (Berlin: de Gruyter, 1974), p. 247. However, Kant's clarification of the absolute position of a thing both in *The Only Premise* and the *Critique of Pure Reason* leaves no room for such a distinction, as I will show below.

20   Another example is M. Heidegger. He reads Kant's "Refutation of Idealism" such that it means to provide an answer to the question of the reality of the external world. See M. Heidegger, *Being and Time*, trans. by J. Macquarrie and E. Robinson (New York: Harper & Row, 1962), pp. 202-08 (marginal pagination of the seventh German edition). But clearly, in the "Refutation of Idealism" (*Kritik der reinen Ver-nunft*, B274-276) Kant is not at all concerned with the *reality*, but with the *actuality* (*Dasein, Existenz*) of objects in space outside of us, instead: "The mere, but empirically determined, consciousness of my own existence (*Dasein*) proves the existence (*Dasein*) of objects in space outside of me" (B275). For Kant, the concern for the *reality* of the external world would be a different sort of thing. Of course, Heidegger's use of "reality" is all right, as long as he remains aware of and indicates its difference from Kant's use when discussing Kantian texts.

21   For the similarities and differences between the distinctions of Kant and Suarez, see my paper, "Kant's Thesis About Being Anticipated by Suarez?" *op. cit.*

22   I. Kant, *Kritik der reinen Vernunft*, B626, and *Kritik der Urteilskraft* (2nd ed.), *Akademie Ausgabe*, vol. 5, pp. 401-2. See also *Beweisgrund*, p. 72ff. For *Bestimmung*,

see *Kritik der reinen Vernunft,* B626. For *"Merkmal,"* see *Beweisgrund,* p. 73-74. The example given is in both places God's omnipotence. For "outside their concepts," see *Kritik der reinen Vernunft,* B627, and *Kritik der Urteilskraft,* p. 402.

23   See, for instance, J. Shaffer, "Existence, Predication, and the Ontological Argument" (originally in *Mind,* 1962), in *The First Critique: Reflections on Kant's Critique of Pure Reason,* ed. by T. Penelhum and J. J. MacIntosh (Belmont: Wadsworth, 1969), p. 127.

24   Franciscus Suarez, *Disputationes metaphysicae* (Salamanca, 1597), disp. 31, sect. 1, no. 3 (hereafter 31.1.3), in Franciscus Suarez, *Opera Omnia,* ed. by C. Berton, vol. 26 (Paris: Vives, 1866), reprinted Hildesheim: Georg Olms, 1965: "Prima [opinio de existentia creaturae] est, existentiam esse rem quamdam distinctam omnino realiter ab entitate essentiae creaturae. Haec existimatur esse opinio D. Thomae, quam in hoc sensu secuti sunt fere omnes antiqui Thomistae" [e.g., Capreolus, Cajetanus, Ferrariensis, Soncinas, Javellus, and Aegidius].

25   Ibid., 31.1.3-10.

26   Ibid., 31.6.1ff (especially 23-24), and 31.7.1ff. See also my paper, "Kant's Thesis About Being Anticipated by Suarez?" *op. cit.*

27   See, for instance, J. Gredt, *Elementa Philosophiae Aristotelico-Thomisticae,* 6th ed. (Freiburg: Herder, 1932), vol. 2, pp. 101-12. Gredt claims that the distinction between existence and essence is a "real distinction, i.e., a *"distinctio realis inter duas realitates positivas intrinsecas"* (p. 104). And he holds, like Wolff, as I will show below, that actuality is a "complement" or "perfection" which the essence as possibility may or may not "receive": "Sed concipimus existentiam realiter distinctam ab essentia tamquam actum ultimum complentem et perficientem essentiam, et essentiam tamquam potentiam realem quae rerecipit existentiam" (p. 102).

28   See F. Suarez, *Disputationes metaphysicae,* 31.6.13-15, 23-24, and 31.7.1ff (significantly, Suarez believes God to be an exception). Also, I. Kant, *Beweisgrund,* p. 72, and *Kritik der reinen Vernunft,* B628.

29   See F. Suarez, *Disputationes metaphysicae,* 31.7.4-5.

30   I. Kant, *Kritik der reinen Vernunft,* B628, and *Beweisgrund,* p. 72.

31   See F. Suarez, *Disputationes metaphysicae,* 31.7.5, and my paper, "Kant's Thesis About Being Anticipated by Suarez?" *op. cit.,* p. 518 n. 4.

32   See J. Shaffer, "Existence, Predication, and the Ontological Argument," *op. cit.,* p. 126, and J. Hintikka, "Kant on Existence, Predication, and the Ontological Argument," *op. cit.,* p. 133. See also L. W. Beck, *Early German Philosophy,* p. 454. Others, like S. Morris Engel, "Kant's 'Refutation' of the Ontological Argument" (originally in *Philosophy and Phenomenological Research,* 1963-64), in *Kant: A Collection of Critical Essays,* ed. by R. P. Wolff (Garden City: Doubleday Anchor, 1967), realize that "Kant does not say 'Being is not a predicate,' he only says it is not a *real* predicate" (p. 194). But instead of looking for help in Kant's other writings, e.g., *The Only Premise,* and in the writings of those whom Kant explicitly criticizes, he develops in a *purely speculative* manner a theory of language and predication for Kant which is meant to make Kant's claim that being is not a real predicate conceptually transparent but, as a matter of fact, merely serves to dismiss it as a mistake (cf. p. 206). This is a perfect example of understanding Kant out of context!

33   See I. Kant, *Beweisgrund*, p. 72F.

34   I. Kant, *Kritik der reinen Vernunft*, B626.

35   I. Kant, *Beweisgrund*, p. 73.

36   I. Kant, *Kritik der reinen Vernunft*, B626.

37   I. Kant, *Beweisgrund*, p. 73.

38   It can also signify, for instance, the relation between pure fictions (*Undinge*). Kant gives as an example, "The God of Spinoza is subject to endless change," *Beweisgrund*, p. 73.

39   I. Kant, *Beweisgrund*, pp. 73-75, and *Kritik der reinen Vernunft*, B626f.

40   I. Kant, *Kritik der reinen Vernunft*, B627, and *Kritik der Urtheilskraft*, p. 402.

41   I. Kant, *Beweisgrund*, p. 73.

42   Ibid.

43   I. Kant, *Kritik der reinen Vernunft*, B267-73, and B287 and note.

44   Ibid., B273-74, and B287 and note.

45   I. Kant, *Beweisgrund*, pp. 74, 75. See also I. Kant, *Kritik der reinen Vernunft*, B267-68, B301-2, and B624 and note.

46   I. Kant, *Kritik der reinen Vernunft*, B302f, and also 1st or A edition, *Akademie Ausgabe*, vol. 4, A244-45.

47   Ibid., B269.

48   Ibid., B628. The German text, without a comma after *überhaupt* and before *nichts fehlt*, allows (and the context requires) that one reads *überhaupt nichts fehlt*, rather than, as does Smith, *eines Dinges Überhaupt*. The preceding sentence reads: "When, therefore, I think a being (*ein Wesen*) as the supreme reality, without any defect (*ohne Mangel*), the question still remains whether it exists or not."

49   Ibid.

50   Ibid., B265-87.

51   Ibid., B265.

52   Ibid., B266.

53   Ibid.

54   Ibid.

55   Ibid., B286.

56   Ibid., (emphasis added).

57   See also Kant's summary of his earlier explanation of being as absolute position, *Beweisgrund*, p. 75: "Um daher in einer so subtilen Vorstellung alles zusammen zu fassen, was die Verwirrung verhüten kann, so sage ich: in einem Existirenden

wird nichts mehr gesetzt als in einem blos Möglichen (denn alsdann ist die Rede von den Prädicaten desselben), allein durch etwas Existirendes wird mehr gesetzt als durch ein blos Mögliches, denn dieses geht auch auf absolute Position der Sache selbst. Sogar ist in der blossen Möglichkeit nicht die Sache selbst, sondern es sind blosse Beziehungen von Etwas zu Etwas nach dem Satze des Widerspruchs gesetzt, und es bleibt fest, dass das Dasein eigentlich gar kein Prädicat von irgend einem Dinge sei."

58   I. Kant, *Kritik der reinen Vernunft*, B272-74.

59   Ibid., B627f.

60   See footnote 57.

61   I. Kant, *Beweisgrund*, p. 76-77.

62   Ibid., p. 76. Kant gives no reference. But see Christian Wolff, *Philosophia prima sive Ontologia* (rev. ed. of 1736 in a modern reprint), in C. Wolff, *Gesammelte Werke*, vol. 3, ed. by J. Ecole (Hildesheim: Georg Olms, 1962), no. 174, p. 143 (hereafter *Ontologia*).

63   C. Wolff, *Ontologia*, no. 85, p. 65: "Possibile est, quod nullam contradictionem involvit seu, quod non est impossibile. — Etenim ex eo, quod quid nullam contradictionem involvit, concluditur, quod non sit impossibile (no. 79)." For the *theological* assumptions underlying this identification of the possibility of a thought with the possibility of a thing, see my paper, "Kant's Thesis About Being Anticipated by Suarez?" *op. cit.*, pp. 513-16.

64   Ibid., no. 59, p. 41: "Aliquid est, cui notio aliqua respondet."

65   Ibid., no. 57, p. 40: "Nihilum dicimus, cui nulla respondet notio."

66   Ibid., no. 59, p. 41.

67   For this etymological interpretation among the scholastics, see F. Suarez, *Disputationes metaphysicae*, in *Opera Omnia*, vol. 25, 3.2.5-6.

68   C. Wolff, *Ontologia*, no. 243, p. 196: "Quicquid est vel esse posse concipitur, dicitur res, quatenus est alizuid: ut adeo res definiri possit per id, quod est aliquid."

69   See F. Suarez, *Disputationes metaphysicae*, 2.4.2: "res quidditative praedicatur." See also 2.4.14-15, where Suarez endorses and argues for Domingo de Soto's claim, and 3.2.4, where he refers to Thomas Aquinas and Avicenna.

70   C. Wolff, *Ontologia*, no. 243, p. 196: "Unde & realitas & quidditas apud scholasticos synonyma sunt — E.gr. Arbor & ens dicitur, & res: ens scilicet, si existentiam respicis; res vero, si quidditatem, sive quod sit aliquid, aut determinata quaedam notio eidem respondeat (no. 59)."

71   His *Disputationes metaphysicae* were used as the compendium of traditional metaphysics and as a textbook at Protestant universities. Suarez himself was acknowledged as the "grandfather" and the "pope" among metaphysicians. For references see M. Grabmann, "Die Disputationes metaphysicae des Franz Suarez in ihrer methodischen Eigenart und Fortwirkung" (1917), republished in M. Grabmann, *Mittelalterliches Geistesleben. Abhandlungen zur Geschichte der Scholastik und Mystik*, vol. 1 (Munich:

Hueber Verlag, 1926), p. 538-39. Also E. Lewalter, *Spanisch-jesuitische und deutsch-lutherische Metaphysik des 17. Jahrhunderts* (Hamburg: Ibero-Amerikanisches Institut, 1935), p. 17, note 3; and L. W. Beck, *Early German Philosophy*, p. 123. Wolff frequently refers to Suarez explicitly, and his definitions, distinctions, etc., are easily recognized as being borrowed from Suarez. To get a first impression, see the entries in the various author's and editor's indices in the *Ontologia*.

72   See F. Suarez, *Disputationes metaphysicae*, 3.2.4: "nam res et ens juxta communem usum tanquam synonyma usurpantur."

73   C. Wolff, *Ontologia*, no. 171, p. 141: "Quod possibile est, id non ideo existit."

74   Ibid., no. 173, p. 142: "Praeter possibilitatem entis aliud quid requiritur, ut existat."

75   Ibid.

76   Ibid., no. 174, p. 143: "Hinc Existentiam definio per complementum possibilitatis. . . . Dicitur existentia etiam Actualitas."

77   Ibid. It will be explained more specifically in the special disciplines. The reason for the existence of the universe, for instance, is demonstrated in theology.

78   Alexander Gottlieb Baumgarten, *Metaphysica*, 7th ed. of 1779 reprinted (Hildesheim: Georg Olms, 1963).

79   A. G. Baumgarten, *Metaphysica*, no. 55, p. 15-16: "Existentia . . . est complexus affectionum in aliquo compossibilium i.e. complementum essentiae sue possibilitatis internae, quatenus haec tantum, vt complexus determinationum spectatur." For the definition of *affectiones* as determinations, see no. 41, p. 13.

80   Ibid., no. 53, p. 15.

81   Ibid., no. 54, p. 15: "Possibile praeter essentiam . . . aut est determinatum, qua omnes affectiones etiam in ipso compossibilies, aut minus. . . . Illud est ACTUALE, hoc NON ENS. . . . PRIVATIVUM (mere possibile) vocatur."

82   Ibid., no. 36, p. 11: "Quae determinando ponuntur in aliquo, (notae et praedicata) sunt DETERMINATIONES, altera positiva, et affirmativa . . . quae si vere sit, est REALITAS. . . ."

83   See ibid., no. 66, p. 18: "Existentia non repugnat essentiae, sed est realitas . . . cum ea compossibilis," and no. 810, p. 332: "Existentia est realitas cum essentia & reliquis realitatibus compossibilis. . . ."

84   L. W. Beck, *Early German Philosophy*, p. 284.

85   I. Kant, *Beweisgrund*, p. 76.

86   Ibid.

87   I. Kant, *Kritik der reinen Vernunft*, B628.

88   For this particular point, see F. Suarez, *Disputationes metaphysicae*, 31.2.6 & 9, and also, for the more systematic critique of the "realist" interpretation of existence, 31.6 and 7.

W. H. WERKMEISTER

What Did Kant Say
And What Has He Been Made to Say?

I take it to be axiomatic that any translation is *ipso facto* also an interpretation of the translated text. I mention this merely in order to forestall any purely philological conception of the theme with which I am here concerned. To be sure, a purely philological problem is at times difficult enough — especially so when the sentences to be translated are long and involved, and when some of the key terms may have various meanings. To remain true in translation to the finer nuances and overtones of the original text is perhaps an even more challenging problem — and it is particularly so when we deal with some of Kant's formulations.

If I am right in maintaining that a translation is *ipso facto* an interpretation of the translated text, then a successful translation presupposes that the translator understands the point of view of the author he translates, and understands also what the author had to say in defending his point of view. In this perspective, Norman Kemp Smith's translation of Kant's *Critique of Pure Reason,* fine as it is in many respects, suffers from the translator's conviction that Kant's *opus* is but a "patchwork." This "patchwork theory" hardly indicates a profound understanding of Kant's first *Critique.* But, of course, other translators of Kantian texts have also encountered difficulties — difficulties which they have not always been able to overcome. I shall here view some of the difficulties in perspective and shall attempt to render the translations more adequate or closer to Kant's intention.

W. H. Werkmeister is professor of philosophy (emeritus), Florida State University, Tallahassee.

1

Let us begin with something which at first glance must seem a mere trifle, but which is actually rather crucial.

Throughout the *Critique of Pure Reason* Kant speaks of *Erkenntnis*, which Kemp Smith consistently translates as *knowledge*. Is this really a trifle? Let us consider what is involved.

The German language distinguishes between *kennen* (from which *Kenntnis* is derived) and *erkennen* (from which we get *Erkenntnis*). *Kennen* means "to know," and *Kenntnis* is the fact of knowing or knowledge. *Erkennen*, however, means "to cognize," and *Erkenntnis* therefore means "cognition"—"the act or process of knowing in the broadest sense." And let us keep in mind that the *Critique of Pure Reason* is not a work in metaphysics and therefore does not even pretend to give us metaphysical knowledge. It is, by Kant's own statement, a work in "transcendental philosophy"; and Kant calls "all cognition transcendental which concerns itself not so much with objects as with the mode of our cognition of objects insofar as this is to be possible *a priori*"(B25).

When we take this into consideration and write *cognition* where Kemp Smith says *knowledge*, certain difficulties of translation—including controversies about Kantian intentions and statements—disappear.

2

Consider, first of all, the controversy over the existence or non-existence of "synthetic *a priori* propositions." Presumably Kant's problem was: "How are synthetic *a priori* judgments possible" (B73)?[1] The translation suggests, if it does not actually imply, that both "synthetic" and *a priori* have adjectival meaning. Most critics of Kant's position, accepting this meaning as basic, have denied the possibility of there being any "synthetic *a priori* propositions."

In his Introduction to Kant's *Critique of Practical Reason*, Lewis White Beck states, "Before Kant, 'a priori synthetic judgments' would have been considered a *contradictio in adjecto*,"[2] and then he raises the question: "Can Kant's Synthetic Judgments be made Analytic?"[3] But when, in view of modern developments in mathematics, we attempt to do so, "do we not at the same time overlook or destroy everything distinctive in (Kant's) theory of empirical knowledge" (p. 22)?

Stephen Körner speaks of Kant's "inquiry into the nature and function of synthetic *a priori* judgments"[4] and makes it quite clear that he believes Kant regards both "synthetic" and *a priori* to be adjectives of judgments and propositions (p. 25).

From Feigl we learn that "all forms of empiricism agree in repudiating the existence of synthetic *a priori* knowledge."[5] And C. I. Lewis, denying the possibility of "synthetic *a priori* truths," found that the problem of the existence of synthetic *a priori* knowledge "is a dead, or nearly dead, issue; conviction that all *a priori* truth is analytic being now quite general."[6]

This is neither the place nor the time to go into further details of the controversy or to consider the various arguments against what is, presumably, the Kantian position. I refer instead to Oliver A. Johnson's article "Denial of the Synthetic *A Priori*."[7] It is my intention to make clear what Kant himself actually said.

3

Kant knew, of course, that "the principle of contradiction must be recognized as the completely sufficient principle of all analytic knowledge." But he knew also that, beyond the sphere of analytical knowledge, this principle has "no authority and no field of application" (A151/B191). Actual experience transcends and must transcend the range of merely analytic propositions. It depends upon sense data that are given, and upon our integrative conception and interpretation of those data. As Kant put it: "Experience is . . . the first product to which our understanding gives rise, in working up the raw material of sensory impressions" (A1). And: "It may well be that even our empirical cognition is a composite (*ein Zusammengesetztes*) of which we receive through impressions and of what our own faculty of cognition . . . supplies from itself" (B1). What our own faculty of cognition supplies are synthetic judgments made *a priori*, and propositions expressing these judgments. They are *a priori*, "not merely because they provide the grounds of other judgments, but also because they are not themselves grounded in higher and more universal modes of cognition" (A148/B188).

What is true in the case of ordinary experience, so Kant maintains, is true also in the case of all sciences and in metaphysics. In fact, all cognition depends ultimately upon synthetic or "ampliative" principles known or accepted *a priori* (A9-10/B13). And right here the question arises: Are there any integrative or synthetic judgments that serve as *a priori* ground of experience? Kant, as we know, answered this question in the affirmative, and then asked: How are they possible?

And here the problem of translation arises; for, in his translation of the *Critique of Pure Reason,* Norman Kemp Smith renders the question as "How are *a priori* synthetic judgments possible" (B19); and throughout the *Critique* he has Kant speak of "*a priori* synthetic judgments" (A9/B13), of "synthetic *a priori* judgments" (B73; A154/B193); (A158/B197), of "*a priori* synthetic propositions" (A39/B56), of "*a priori* synthetic knowledge" (A782/B810), and of "synthetic *a priori* principles" (A248/B305). These formulations all imply that both "synthetic" and *a priori* are adjectival in meaning, modifying judgments, propositions, and principles. Kant's own statements, however, do not warrant this interpretation. He thus asks (B19): "Wie sind synthetische Urteile a priori möglich?"; and (B73): "Wie sind synthetische Sätze a priori möglich?" The *a priori* here modifies neither "judgments" nor "propositions" but their being possible.

Kant's intention is even more evident in such formulations as "Auf solche Weise sind synthetische Urteile a priori möglich" (A158/B197), and ". . . machen synthetische Sätze a priori möglich" (A39/B56). It is here obvious that, for Kant, the term *a priori* has adverbial rather than adjectival meaning.[8]

Of course, there are also passages in the *Critique of Pure Reason* that make it impossible even for Kemp Smith to use *a priori* as an adjective. We thus read (A718/B746): "We are here concerned . . . with those synthetic propositions that can be known *a priori*": and (A782/B810): "If I am to pass *a priori* beyond the concept of an object . . . ."

4

To be sure, the principle of contradiction is "the universal and completely sufficient principle of all analytic cognition" (A151/B191), and is itself known analytically. It is also sufficient as basis for (Aristotelian) logic; for if "all A is B, and all B is C, then all A is C." But pure logic is not sufficient for the development of a science of nature, or even of geometry as "a science which determines the properties of space synthetically, and yet *a priori*" (A25/B40). This is so because geometry depends upon certain synthetic propositions which we accept *a priori*. In conformity with the usage of his times, Kant called such propositions axioms (A163/B204). Today, we call them postulates. But the function of these "fundamental propositions" is clearly the same.

To make his point, Kant argued "that the straight line between two points is the shortest, is a synthetic proposition. For my concept of *straight* contains nothing of quantity, but only quality" (B16). To be sure, we might regard the Kantian proposition as simply the definition of "straight line." But this is an objection to an example only, not to the Kantian thesis as such. To convince yourself of this, consider Euclid's fifth postulate in its most common form: "To a given straight line one and only one parallel line can be drawn through a point not on the given line."9 Surely this postulate is a synthetic proposition, and an indispensable presupposition of the whole of Euclidean plane geometry. In this sense it is *a priori* to the system as a whole.

When we retain the definition of the straight line as the shortest distance between two points but modify the fifth postulate to read that to a given straight line *no* line can be drawn parallel through a point not on the given line, we can still develop a consistent system of geometry; but it will be the Riemannian form of noneuclidian geometry which, in effect, is the geometry of spherical rather than plane surfaces. And when we identify the straight line (defined as the shortest distance between two points) with the path of a ray of light, we have transformed the definition into a postulate, and the resultant geometry is that of the Einsteinian universe—a system that depends just as much as any other system upon its postulates or principles *a priori*.

In a similar sense, any natural science—such as physics—"contains synthetic judgments [accepted] *a priori* as principles" (B17). As Kant put it: "The laws of nature . . . , one and all, without exception, stand under higher principles of understanding" and these are accepted *a priori* (A159/B198). Or as he also stated: "There are certain laws which first make a nature possible, and these laws are *a priori*"(A216/B263).

Consider but two examples of such principles: (1) Kant's "Second Law of Mechanics" (which is actually Newton's First Law of Motion): "Every change of matter has an external cause."10 (2) Kant's "Third Law of Mechanics" (Newton's Third Law of Motion): "In all communication of motion, action and reaction are always equal to one another" (Reference 10, AA544, p. 106).

No one can seriously doubt the synthetic character of these basic "laws." Nor can anyone question the crucial role they play as foundation stones or principles *a priori* for the whole system of Newtonian mechanics—the system for which Kant sought to provide the cognitive basis.

In Kant's *Critique of the Faculty of Judgment*, we find further confirmation of the adverbial meaning of the *a priori*. To give but one example:

"So far as reason has to do with nature, as the complex of objects of external sense, it can base itself partly upon laws which the understanding itself prescribes *a priori* to nature."[11]

When C. I. Lewis now maintains that "there are no synthetic statements which can be known true *a priori*" (*Analysis,* p. ix), he overlooks Kant's explicit statement that the criterion of any cognitive system, and therefore of its *a priori* principles, consists in "the *truth* of the consequences that can be deduced from it (their accordance with themselves and with experience); and finally, in the completeness of the ground of explanation of these consequences which, carrying us back . . . in an *a posteriori* analytic manner give us an account with what has previously been thought in a synthetic *a priori* manner" (B115). Or, as Kant also put it: "The possibility of experience is what gives objective reality to all our *a priori* modes of cognition. . . . Experience depends upon *a priori* principles . . . whose objective reality, as necessary conditions of experience, and indeed of its very possibility, can always be shown in experience. Apart from this relation synthetic principles *a priori* are completely impossible" (A157/B196). All of this simply means that the truth of the synthetic principles that are accepted *a priori* is established *a posteriori* by their empirically ascertainable consequences.

5

In a literal sense the translation of *Anschauung* as *intuition* is correct, for *Anschauung* — derived from *anschauen,* to look at, to view directly, to contemplate — strictly speaking means an immediate and non-inferential cognition. *Intuition* — Latin *intuitus,* from *intueri,* pp. of *intueor* — has the same meaning. All this is clear and indisputable. But there are ambiguities in the text of the first *Critique* that require clarification.

We read, for example (A19/B33), that "intuition takes place only insofar as the object (*Gegenstand*) is given to us." But objects, so Kant immediately adds, "are *thought* through the understanding" rather than intuited. Our thinking then is merely occasioned by what is given us through the senses, and what is given us through the senses are sense impressions only.

The confusion in all of this arises from Kant's ambivalent reference to "the object of empirical intuition"; for the term "object" suggests more than a mere sense impression — even when Kant calls the "indefinite object of empirical intuition" an "appearance." We are all familiar with the difficulties of interpreting the relation of an appearance to the object of which it is an appearance. The problem is of sufficient seriousness to require clarification now.

Let us suppose that, having previously closed my eyes, I now open them and immediately and directly see a "patch of red." I intuit the "red" which, as sensory content of intuition, is an appearance. But that "patch of red" has a "shape" of some kind—angular rather than round, let us say; and I immediately intuit that shape also (if ever so vaguely). Moreover, I intuit the occurrence of that "red patch" as being simultaneous and/or in sequential order with other sense impressions. Although entirely noninferential, my intuition is already complex in a threefold sense. It involves (a) the sensory quale "red," (b) the spatial form of the quale, and (c) the temporal aspect under which alone I have the intuition of the "red patch."

All of this is obvious and clear; and since our intuition of a "patch of red" is generically representative of all sensible intuitions, we may readily grant Kant's thesis that spatiality and temporality are the *forms* of sensible intuitions in general—spatiality being "the *form* of all appearances of outer sense" (A26/B42), and temporality being "the *form* of inner sense" (A33/B49). But when Kant now states that "space is represented as an infinite *given* magnitude" (A25/B39), and that "time is a necessary representation that underlies all intuition" (A31/B46), he obviously goes beyond intuition proper and sets forth a thesis that must be based upon other considerations. For Kant, it actually is a matter of *Vorstellung*. And now we face again a problem of translation.

6

The German term *Vorstellung* is rather ambiguous—as is also the English term "representation." As a rule, the meaning depends in each case on context. *Vorstellung* may thus mean a theatrical performance, a presentation at court, an introduction of one person to another, a remonstrance—to mention but a few of the meanings and to illustrate their diversity. In addition, however, the term *Vorstellung* is used also in such formulations as *sich eine Vorstellung davon machen* (to form an idea or notion of something), and *eine Vorstellung davon haben* (to have a conception, notion, or image of something). It is in this latter sense that Kant uses the term.

To be sure, the English term *representation*, being perhaps even more ambiguous, has meanings not even included in the range of meanings of *Vorstellung*: "the action or fact of one person standing for another as to legal rights and obligations," "something that represents — such as a likeness, a model, or a picture." But, of course, the English term also means *an act or process by which the mind forms an image or an object;*[12] and it is in this last sense that the term "representation" does in fact correspond to Kant's employment of *Vorstellung*.

What is crucial is that, as a translation of *Vorstellung,* the term "representation" must be taken primarily as suggestive of an act — be that an act of intuiting or of thinking; and that it must be taken secondarily as designating that which one intuits or thinks. The specific meaning depends in each case entirely on the context within which the term is being used. It may be helpful, therefore, to abandon the rigid and stereotypical translation of *Vorstellung* as "representation," and to use terms such as "idea," "notion," "conception," or "image," as is textually required.[13]

Kant himself provides the ground for such flexible translation, for he explicitly states that "there is no lack of terms suitable for each kind of *Vorstellung*" so that "we should not needlessly encroach upon the province of any one of them" (A320/B376f). There is, of course, the term *Vorstellung* in the generic sense; and here Kant himself uses the Latin *repraesentatio* (from *re-praesento,* to make present, set in view, exhibit, display, depict). Subordinate to it are "perception," "sensation," and "cognition" — the latter being either "intuition" or "concept." A "pure" concept (one that has its origin exclusively in the understanding), Kant calls a "notion." A concept formed from notions which transcend experience is a concept of reason or an *idea.* All of these special terms are, according to Kant, part of the range of meanings of *Vorstellung.* The term "representation" hardly does justice to them all.

A few quotations from the first *Critique* — in which I shall introduce what I regard as the proper substitutes — will suffice to substantiate my point.

1 "Since all representations (*Vorstellungen* = cognitions), whether they have for their objects outer things or not, belong, in themselves, as determinations of the mind, to our inner state" (A34/B50).

2 "The representation (*Vorstellung* = image) of a body in intuition . . . contains nothing that can belong to an object itself, but merely the appearance of something" (A44/B61).

3 "The judgment is therefore the mediate cognition (*Erkenntnis*) of an object, and thus the representation (*Vorstellung* = cognition) of a representation (*Vorstellung* = conception) of it" (A68/B93).

4 "Since we have to deal with the manifold of our representations (*Vorstellungen* = sensations), and since the object which corresponds to them means nothing to us . . . the unity which the object makes necessary can be nothing else than the formal unity of consciousness in the synthesis of the manifold of representations (*Vorstellungen* = sensations)" (A105).

5 "The manifold representations (*Vorstellungen* = images) which are given in an intuition, would not be one and all *my* representations (*Vorstellungen* = images), if they did not all belong to one self-consciousness" (B132).

6 "The thought that the representations (*Vorstellungen* = images) given in intuition one and all belong to me, is therefore equivalent of the thought that I unite them in one self-consciousness . . . and although this thought is not itself the consciousness of the *synthesis* of the representations (*Vorstellungen* = concepts), it presupposes the possibility of that synthesis" (B134).

7 "We have representations (*Vorstellungen* = notions) in us and can become conscious of them. . . . How, then, does it come about that we posit an object for these representations (*Vorstellungen* = notions)?" (A197/B242).

8 "When I perceive that something happens, this representation (*Vorstellung* = perception) first of all contains that there is something preceding . . ." (A198/B243).

9 "External objects (bodies), however, are mere appearances, and are therefore nothing but a species of my representations (*Vorstellungen* = images), the objects of which are something only through these (*Vorstellungen* = images)" (A370).

10 "There are only two possible ways in which synthetic representations (*Vorstellungen* = cognitions) and their objects can establish connection . . ." (A92/124).

11 "From this it then follows that appearances in general are nothing outside our representations (*Vorstellungen* = images)" (A507/B535).

12 "This ideal of an *ens realissimum,* although it is indeed a mere representation (*Vorstellung* = idea), is first realized " (A583/B611$_n$).

Since the twelve examples come from various parts of the *Critique,* I regard them as typical for Kant's use of the term *Vorstellung* in its various connotations to establish my point.

7

There is, however, one other problem that requires my special attention. Briefly stated it is this: Since the term "representation" also means (as *Vorstellung* does not) the action or fact of standing for or representing something, it is easy to assume that even in the Kantian view a *Vorstellung* = representation must represent something — namely, the *Ding an sich.*

It is not necessary at this time to review the wide-ranging controversy involving the conception of the thing in itself. Anyone interested in some of the discussions and arguments may find Gisela Shaw's *Das Problem des Dinges an sich in der englischen Kantinterpretation*[14] most helpful. W. H. Walsh was perhaps not too far off the mark when he said that the thing in itself is "without doubt a sorry bugbear for Kantians."[15] The confusion is increased beyond all bounds when T. D. Weldon asserts that, "strictly speaking, the *noumenon* is the concept of a thing in itself, and the thing in itself is the alleged object of which the noumenon is a concept."[16]   What, then, are we to make of the thing in itself?

Let us remember that in the scholastic tradition of metaphysics — of which Baumgarten's *Metaphysica* is a representative example with which Kant was thoroughly familiar — the idea of *res per se* was a common conception. Kant's term *Ding an sich* is, in effect, but a translation of the Latin term. But it is significant that the Latin *res per se* consistently appears in phrases such as *res per se considerata* and *res per se spectata* — that is, "things considered in themselves" and "things viewed in themselves." *Res per se* and *Ding an sich* are thus but abridgments of the original phrases — abridgments which, nevertheless, retain at least implicitly the sense of the extended original.

When we now turn to the *Critique of Pure Reason,* we find that Kant himself speaks of a "distinction . . . between things as objects of experience and those same things as things in themselves" (Bxxvii), and of "objects *as they appear* and *as they are*" (A258/B313). But the distinction does not imply that Kant here speaks of two different entities, for he specifically states that the distinction is "between things as objects of experience and "those same things" as things in themselves"; and he speaks also of "*viewing* objects from two different points of view" (Bxviii$_n$).

To be sure, there are statements in the *Critique of Pure Reason* which at first glance appear to contradict this thesis. We read, for example, that, "while much can be said *a priori* as regards the form of appearances, nothing whatsoever can be asserted of the thing itself, which may underlie those appearances" (A49/B66). And: "As soon as we take away our subjective constitution, the represented (*vorgestellte* = imagined) object, with the characteristic qualities which sensible intuition attributes to it, is nowhere to be found, nor can it be found; for it is [our] subjective constitution which determines the form of the object as appearance" (A44/B62). Again: "How things may be in themselves, apart from the representations (*Vorstellungen* =

perceptions) through which they affect us, is entirely outside our sphere of cognition" (A190/B235).

When we view such passages—and others that could be added—in context, we find that the thing-in-itself as an unknowable entity is the projection of a reason that strives to transcend all limits of possible experience (A131/B171f). Although we cannot think an object save through categories—but reason can and does employ them—"we cannot cognize an object so thought save through intuitions corresponding to these concepts" (B165).

In order to see clearly what is involved here, we must keep in mind that Kant quite sharply distinguished "transcendental *realism*"—advocates of which, being dualists, "interpret outer appearances . . . as things-in-themselves, that exist independently of us and of our sensibility" (A369)—from his own position, which he identified as "transcendental *idealism*" according to which "external things exist as well as I myself exist" but are, nevertheless, "mere appearances, and are therefore nothing but species of my representations (*Vorstellungen* = perceptual objects)" (A370f). "The understanding can never transcend those limits of sensibility within which alone objects can be given to us" (A246/B303). To speak of "things-in-themselves" which, presumably, transcend these limits, "is impossible" (A276/B332). I know nothing about such things, "nor do I need to know, since a thing can never come before me except in appearance" (A277/B333).

However, we must remember that the categories "extend further than sensible intuition" (A251) and that therefore we are able to think objects which, at the moment, are not objects of our sensibility but which, nevertheless, may become such objects. When we speak of them as "real things prior to our perceiving them" this is quite legitimate if it means that "in the advance of experience we must meet with such a perception" (A493/B521).

Similarly, we may speak of "the real things of past time" if "a regressive series of possible perceptions in accordance with empirical laws . . . provides the possibility of extending the chain of experience from the present perception back to the conditions which determine this perception in respect of time" (A495/B523).

Finally, when we think of nature as "the sum of appearances insofar as they stand . . . in thoroughgoing interaction"—that is, when we view nature "as a dynamical whole"—we are concerned "with the unity in the *existence* of appearances" (A419/B446f). This unity means that "all appearances stand in thoroughgoing connection according to necessary laws" (A114; A216/B263). Insofar as these laws are empirical, they "cannot in their specific character be *derived* from the categories" (B165). To be sure, even the empirical laws presuppose as their ultimate ground the broad principle that "everything that happens is determined *a priori* through its cause within the [realm of] appearance" (A227/B280); but the necessity intrinsic to the empirically discernible special laws of nature is not dependent upon our sense impressions, nor is it directly derivable from the pure understanding (A127). It is intrinsic to the interrelations of the appearances themselves (A228/B280).

What bearing does all this have upon the problem of things in themselves? To begin with, we have encountered three distinct cases in which it is quite legitimate to speak of "things" in distinction from their appearance. We have found it to be quite legitimate in terms of Kant's transcendentalism to speak (a) of "real things" prior to their becoming objects of experience; (b) of "real things" of past times; and (c) of discoverable empirical laws that determine the interrelations of the things that constitute the dynamical whole of nature. It is perfectly possible to view all of these things in relation to an experiencing subject and its sensibility. They are then seen as mere appearances. But it is equally possible to contemplate or view them without an explicit reference to actual sense impressions—in which case they may be said to be thought of as things in themselves in an empirical sense.

Kant himself put it this way: "When we say that the senses represent (*vorstellen* = perceive) objects *as they appear,* and the understanding objects *as they are,* the latter statement is to be taken, not in the transcendental, but in the merely empirical meaning of the terms, namely as meaning that the objects must be represented (*vorgestellt* = conceived) as objects of experience, that is, as appearances in thoroughgoing interconnection with one another, and not as they may be apart from their relation to possible experience . . . as objects of the pure understanding" (A258/B313f). And as Kant also puts it—and perhaps more pointedly—appearance "always has two sides, the one by which the object is viewed in and by itself (without regard to the mode of intuiting it—its nature therefore remaining always problematic), the other by which the form of the intuition of this object is taken into account" (A38/B57). In any case we are dealing with one and the same object considered in two distinct perspectives.

NOTES

1 All references to the *Critique of Pure Reason* will be given thus in the text. The pagination is given in the margin of the Norman Kemp Smith translation and corresponds to that of the German text of the *Akademie Ausgabe*.

2 Lewis White Beck, *Kant, Critique of Practical Reason* (Chicago: University of Chicago Press, 1949), p. 9.

3 In Kant, *A Collection of Critical Essays,* ed. by Robert Paul Wolff (Garden City: Doubleday Anchor, 1967), pp. 3-22.

4 Stephan Körner, *Kant* (Baltimore: Penguin, 1955), p. 22.

5 Herbert Feigl, "Logical Positivism," in *Twentieth Century Philosophy,* ed. by D. D. Runes (New York: Philosophical Library, 1947), p. 387.

6 C. I. Lewis, *Analysis of Knowledge and Valuation* (La Salle, Illinois: Open Court, 1946), p. 158.

7 *Philosophy* (July 1960), pp. 1-10.

8 See W. H. Werkmeister, *Kant: The Architectonic and Development of his Philosophy* (La Salle, Illinois: Open Court, 1980), pp. 66-69. See also Robert Paul Wolff's "Introduction" to Lewis White Beck's translation of Kant's *Foundations of the Metaphysics of Morals* (Indianapolis & New York: Bobbs-Merrill, 1969), ixn.

9 See W. H. Werkmeister, *A Philosophy of Science* (New York: Harper, 1940; reprint ed. University of Nebraska, 1965), p. 192.

10 *Die Metaphysischen Anfangsgründe der Naturwissenschaft,* 1786, AA543. Translation by James Ellington, *Metaphysical Foundations of Natural Science* (Indianapolis and New York: Library of Liberal Arts, 1970), p. 104.

11 Immanuel Kant, *The Critique of Judgment,* trans. by James Creed Meredith (Oxford: Clarendon Press, 1928, 1973 reprint), p. 233.

12 The unabridged *Oxford Dictionary.*

13 In his detailed commentary on the *Critique of Pure Reason,* H. J. Paton makes a similar suggestion. See his *Kant's Metaphysica of Experience* (New York: Macmillan, 1936), vol. 1, p. 94 n. 5. But what I am suggesting here goes far beyond Paton's suggestion.

14 *Kant-Studien, Ergänzungsheft* 97 (1969), 177 pages.

15 *Reason and Experience* (Oxford, 1947), p. 11 n. 1.

16 T. D. Weldon, *Introduction to Kant's Critique of Pure Reason,* 2nd ed. (Oxford, 1958), p. 193.

Index

The page numbers entered in bold-face type indicate extended discussions of the topics in the text. References to the footnotes are confined to the informationally important. The Latin and English equivalent of Kant's German have been introduced only when they illuminate the sense of the German original.

RITTER LIBRARY
BALDWIN-WALLACE COLLEGE